A Basketmaker's Odyssey

Over, Under, Around & Through

Written by Lyn Syler
Illustrations and Photography by Carolyn Kemp

The Hands of Rowena Bradley, Cherokee Basketmaker

This book is dedicated to the happy memory of Rowena Bradley, my mentor and friend, who like most Cherokee basketmakers learned "the way" from her mother.

Lyn

"Let the beauty you love
be what you do.
There are hundreds of ways
to kneel and kiss the ground"

Rumi

Published by Word Weavers Ink
Twenty-four basket instructions with full color illustrations

ISBN 0-9771941-1-6
©Lyn Syler and Carolyn Kemp
First Edition
Printed by TSE Worldwide Press

Distributed by Word Weavers Ink
SAN 256-9604
P.O. Box 1214
Matthews NC 28106
WordWeaversInk@Yahoo.com
www.WordWeaversInk.com

Cover art by Carolyn Kemp
Dedicated to her Mother and Father

Acknowledgments:
A special "thank you" to all the basketmakers who contributed their time and
talent to this book; especially Judy Wobbleton, Dianne Kennedy and Jimmie
Kent, whose assistance was invaluable. To our families, we cannot say thank
you enough. Your patience, understanding and support sustained us
throughout this project. And, last but not least, a big thanks to all our proof
readers, especially John!
Lyn and Carolyn

CONTENTS

INTRODUCTION

*T*hrough intent, craft is transformed into spiritual practice. Focus and openness are intertwined, coiled, spiraled into awareness. This form of contemplation quiets the busy mind and weaves us deeper into the Mystery. The decision to create beauty is deliberate and purposeful. The creation of a basket...a vessel... becomes a powerful journey; a mystical process of going Over, Under, Around and Through our smaller self to the greater Self. Inner then manifests as outer. We realize that **we** are the vessel...**we** are the Divine Creative Principle in form. Understanding this, craft becomes more than a creative outlet...it promotes a consciousness of the connectedness of all things. In this way, basketry becomes a catalyst for personal transformation. Through this hands-on spirituality, weaving a basket becomes a prayer.

Deb Teramani RScP
A Spirit inspired artist and RSI Practitioner.

Many years ago, I said "If your basket is not like someone else's, yours is simply blessed with more personality and character....never 'bad'". I still believe that, but I also know that intention is what matters.

How can anything done in an angry or hurtful state of mind turn out well? If you, on the other hand, have the highest good for yourself or someone else in mind as you work, you can make only beautiful baskets, knit only gorgeous scarves and throw only perfect pots.

Dr. Wayne Dyer, in his most recent book, *The Power of Intention*, describes seven "faces" of intention. Would it surprise you that the #1 "face" is creativity? He suggests that it is the "energy of creativity" that brings us from "nowhere" to "now here" and starts us on a path toward our destiny.

For many of us, the creative "face" of intention is our reason for being.

How you stay in touch with your Source is a completely individual thing. Many pray, and prayer takes many forms. For some, prayer must be done in a sanctuary. For many others, meditation opens the channels, freeing your mind to recognize and hear your Energy of Creativity. For others, prayer is as simple as doing while knowing that your intention is aligned with your Source. In this respect, anything and everything you do can be done prayerfully and creatively.

There is a wonderful trend in our society to do everything more mindfully.

One of the instigators of this trend was a great book called *Knitting into the Mystery* by Susan S. Izard and Susan S. Jorgensen. Groups all over the world have been created to knit prayerfully for people who have need of hats, shawls, scarves and most of all prayers.

I suggest to you that basketmakers can make just as impressive a statement to our world by weaving creatively and mindfully. *Over, Under, Around and Through* is my effort to appeal to the creative intention in each and every artisan. There is so much need in our world that weaving, just like knitting, can meet and heal in another person's body and/ or spirit. May my offering to you touch your creative "face" with inspiration, encouragement, and help you on your path to your personal destiny.

Lyn Syler and Sherry C. Baldwin

Basket Class

In "Basket Class" Lyn and her assistant, The Basket Lady, will give you detailed instruction to supplement the directions in the book. Even though the patterns are very complete there are certain techniques that can pose a challenge. This section is designed to help you through those difficult areas.

Cable Cast On:

1. Hold needle with slip knot in left hand. Hold the long loose end in right hand as shown.

Adding a weaver while twining:
As in the photograph, just lay the new weaver beside the old one, on top of a stake and continue twining. Cut the ends to "butt" later when they are dry.

1

2

2. Insert the tip of the right needle into the loop beneath the left needle, front to back.
Wrap the yarn around (counter clockwise) the tip of the right needle.

Adding a weaver (flat material):
When using flat or flat oval material, overlap the ends for four spokes, letting the old one run out on top of a spoke and continuing with the new weaver.

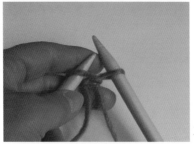

3

3. Using your right index finger for tension, pull the yarn out, leaving a loop on the right needle.

4

4. Transfer the new loop from the right needle to the left needle by inserting the tip of the left needle into the loop from the bottom. Then slide the loop off the right needle onto the left needle.

Adding a weaver (round material):
When doing a plain weave or a three rod wale, crimp (pinch with needle-nose pliers), bend and push the end of the old weaver into the weaving to the left of the next spoke past an "under" stroke. Bend, crimp and push the new weaver into the weaving to the right of the previous spoke.

5

5. Repeat steps 2-4 using the newly made loop on the left needle each time.
Hint: As you do the cable cast-on, do not pull your stitches too tight. They should be loose enough that the needle slips easily beneath each new loop.

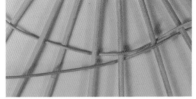

Chase Weaving :
Chase weaving is done with **two** weavers. The first one, referred to as the weaver, weaves over and under for several stakes. Then the chaser weaves over and under for several stakes. The chaser must never catch up with the weaver.

Continuous Weaving with Plain Weave:
With an uneven number of spokes, continuous weaving is possible, i.e. weaving one row after another until the piece runs out. One way to do continuous weaving with an even number of stakes is to weave over **two** stakes at the end of each row. Then the weaving is thrown into an alternate path. This is sometimes called an "Indian Base".

Crimping: To crimp the spokes of round reed, pinch them with needle nose pliers at the base of the spoke, then bend on the crease.

Diagonal Weave: Diagonal weave is done with two like or similar elements at a 45 degree angle.

Ending Weaver on a Round Base: Crimp, bend and push the end of a weaver into the weaving just past an under stroke.

Ending a Start/Stop Row (Twill Weave): By overlapping four pairs of stakes you are hiding the beginning and ending of the weaver in a start/stop row.

Fanning a Corner: There is a large empty area at the corners of square and rectangular basket bases. As you weave around the base, force the stakes to move from the center of the sides (one at a time) toward the corner. By the fourth or fifth row of weaving the base should be a sunburst, with fairly equal spaces between all the stakes.

Forming Feet or Ears on Cat Head Basket: Now pinch the corner stakes together and lift up on the corners as you weave around. As you are holding the corners up and together, pull firmly on the weaver to keep the stakes in place. If the "feet" (or "ears") aren't pronounced enough, place your thumbs in the corners (from the inside) and push the corners out.

Locking Row & Mitering Flat Reed at Corner: A locking row is woven with a very narrow weaver while the base is flat, opposite the overs/unders of the base. The weaver can continue if you are doing a continuous weave or it can end as a start/stop row. Fold the reed at the corner at a 90 degree angle which reverses sides of the weaver. Mitering keeps the reed square and tight around the corner.

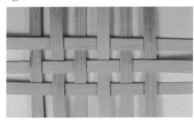

Plain Weave, Over 1, Under 1: Any weave that is over 1, under 1, with like or unlike materials.

Randing: Weaving over one and under one with an odd number of stakes.

Right and Wrong Side of Reed: The right side of reed, the side you normally want on the outside of your basket, is smooth to the touch and should have no "hairs". The wrong side of reed, on the other hand, when bent over your finger becomes very "hairy" and is much less attractive than the right side.

Weaving a Twill Base: If you will remember Over 2, Over 1, Under 2, Under 1, you will always be able to weave a 2/2 twill base with or without a pattern. Those are the beginning strokes for the first four rows. After that, the weave is over or under 2's etc., ending the row with a two or a one.

Center

1st 2nd 3rd 4th

Example:

Lay 13 pieces of reed horizontally, no space between them.

Weave the **first piece** in vertically, (to the right of center) from the bottom up, over 2, under 2, over 2, etc., ending with a one (because of the odd number).

Weave the **second piece** in vertically, bottom to top, over 1, under 2, over 2, under 2 etc.

Weave the **third piece** in vertically, bottom to top, under 2, over 2, under 2 etc. (again ending with a one).

Weave the **fourth piece** in vertically, bottom to top, under 1, over 2, under 2, over 2 etc.

Repeat these four rows to the right with half the pieces, then repeat the four rows to the left in reverse. The first row to the left will be a duplicate of row 4.

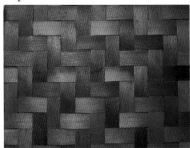

A Completed Twill Base

Rimming Technique: After all the stakes have been tucked and cut and the handle inserted, place a soaked piece of rim material over the false rim on the inside of the basket. Allow 2" - 3" of overlap. Make sure the overlap is pointing to the right. Mark the overlapped area and remove. Shave half the thickness from the top of one side and bottom of the other side, so that the thickness is not greater than a single thickness of rim material.

Replace the inside rim on the basket. Hold it in place with clothespins or clamps. Next place another soaked piece of rim material on the outside, again making sure the overlap is pointing to the right.

Repeat the marking and shaving process. Place the rim back on the basket holding it with clothespins or clamps.

Place a piece of seagrass on top of the rim, between the two rim pieces.

With a long soaked piece of lashing material, lash the rim permanently on the basket. Start by taking one end of the lasher, wrong side up, under the inside rim from bottom to top, down over the false rim row, to the outside of the basket and under the outside rim. Cut it later so that it is even with the bottom of the rim.

With the other end, push the lasher through the next space, now coming around the rim, right side up. Continue lashing in this manner, back to the starting point.

End the lasher in the same place it began, taking it under the seagrass to the outside. When the lasher is dry, cut it even with the bottom of the rim.

Rim - with Pine Needles:

Tie one end of the thread (waxed linen) onto the false rim and thread the tapestry needle with the other end.

Place the pine needles around the rim, over the false rim. Put half on the inside and half on the outside.

Bring the tapestry needle to the outside of the basket and go through the second space between stakes to the inside.

Take the tapestry needle between every second and third stake.

Tighten the thread often.

Adjust the pine needles so the ends are staggered and won't end all at the same time.

Add in a new pine needle every time one runs out by pushing the end up into the core of needles.

Keep the bundle consistently the same size.

When you have gone all the way around the basket you will need to mesh the needles, adjust the bundles and stitch them together Some of the bulk can be reduced by selectively cutting the pine needles to staggered lengths.

When you have reached the beginning stitch, make a couple of back stitches under the false rim between stakes to secure it.

Bring the tapestry needle at an angle up and through the bundle. Cut the thread.

Leave the "ends" on the pine needles or cut them off; it's your choice.

Space Dying: Put several long soaked pieces of reed (or ash/oak) together in a round coil approximately 8'-10" diameter. Have three or four pots of dye heated. Dip one quarter of the coil into the first dye. Let it drip. Turn the coil around and dip the opposite quarter into another dye. Then dip the last two quarters into the other two dyes; let them run a little, blending the colors into each other.

Spaced Dyed Twill Weave

Start/Stop Row Plain Weave: Start the weaver on top of a stake. If it is the first row of weaving, choose a stake that originates from underneath the base weaving. Weave all the way around and when the starting point is reached, weave over the beginning to the fourth stake. Cut the weaver so the end hides behind the fourth stake. No ends should ever show from the outside or the inside of the basket.

Start/Stop Row Twill Weave: Begin the (twill weaving) row on the outside of the basket on top of a set of stakes. Weave all the way around, back to the starting point. Continue to weave over the beginning of the row to the fourth set of stakes. No ends should ever show from the outside or the inside of the basket.

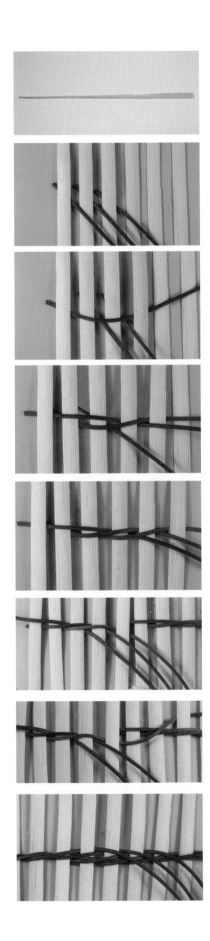

Tapering a Weaver: Tapering means just that...start very thin and gradually grow to the full or normal width of the material.

Three Rod Wale with Step Up:

Place three weavers behind three consecutive spokes.

Take the far left weaver over the next two spokes, behind the third spoke and out to the front.

Again, and every time, pick up the far left weaver, take it to the right, over two spokes and under the third and out.

One complete series of three strokes.

End the wale with the three weavers coming out just to the left of the stake that the first weaver started behind.

Now prepare to do a step up, which is the transition between one row and the next. Bring the farthest right weaver to the right, over two spokes and behind the third and out. Repeat with the other two weavers, using the farthest right weaver each time. The step up is now complete.

Twining with Two Weavers: Start two weavers on two consecutive spokes. *Pick up the top weaver and go behind the next spoke. Repeat from *.

Twining with Folded Weaver: Start two weavers by folding a long piece of weaving material a little off center and looping the fold around a spoke. Always take the top weaver under the next spoke.

Twining with "Full" Twist: In regular twining, a twist is made while going around the spokes. To do a "full" twist make another twist (reversing the order of the top and bottom weavers) before making the final twist around the spoke.

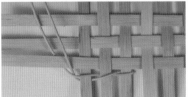

Twining to Lock Base: Sometimes you need to lock a base so it won't move out of place. One way is a plain weave, start/stop locking row. Another is a row of twining. Make the turn around the corners, keeping the top weaver going under the next.

Basic Tools

Upsetting: When using flat stakes dampen each of them at the edge of the base and bend them over upon themselves. When using round spokes, crimp the dampened spoke at the edge of the base and bend it so it stands upright.

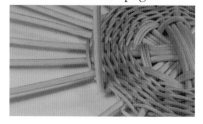

A - Alligator clips
B - Bone awl
C - Needle nose pliers
D - Common pencil
E - Spoke weight
F - Fine cutters
G - Clothespin
H - Round & flat reed gauge
I - Shaver
J - Heavy reed cutters
K - Wood handle awl
L - Cloth tape measure
M - Carving knife

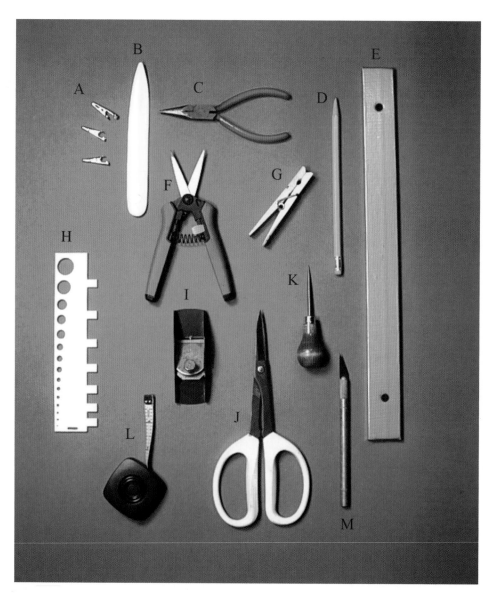

Know Your Materials:

Most of the baskets made in the United States are made of imported reed which is the product of rattan vine. It is cut and sliced into flat, flat-oval, half-round and round reed. It is quite porous, takes dyes readily and is flexible when wet. Oak, Ash, Elm, Hickory, Dogwood, Cedar and Maple are among the native basketmaking woods and are used by basketmakers all over the country. Many varieties of willow and osiers are harvested from the wild as well as grown domestically, specially for basketmaking. Learn to recognize the different kinds of materials in your part of the world and experiment with them in your baskets.

Abenaki Style Knitting Basket

By Dianne Kennedy

Dimensions: 10" high x 6" diameter

Marriage of the basketmaker and the knitter is a natural union and with so much interest in both of these hand crafts, it was only natural for us to include a knitting basket. The "Abenaki" in the title refers to a Native American Indian Tribe from the northeastern United States. Our prototype was an old ash basket that would hold yarn, keep it straight and knot-free, and be portable; the "hole" of the original lid was made of a coiled piece of ash. Dianne used a turned piece of wood, her own cotton braided rag strap and space dyed reed, her specialty. Some things had to be modified, of course, but the authenticity of the design remains.

MATERIALS and PREPARATION

5/8" Flat reed (stakes)

3/8" Flat reed (weavers)

11/64" Dyed and natural flat oval reed (lashing and overlays)

7mm Flat or flat oval reed (for lid false rim) or use 3/8" trimmed to 7mm or ¼"

2 Round reed (chase weaving)

3/8" Flat oval (first rim and lid rim)

Seagrass (rim filler)

2 ¾" Diameter slotted wooden donut ring

5" Diameter slotted wooden base

Dianne's own Braided Rag Strap with loops, or a strap of your choice

    (see "Facts about Contributors" for how to get Dianne's strap)

WEAVING THE BASE:

From the natural 5/8" flat reed, cut 16 pieces 14" long. Taper the ends gradually as in **DIAGRAM 1** making them about 3/8" wide at the narrowest point. Wet the spokes and push the ends into the slot in the base right side up. Space them equally. See **DIAGRAM 2**. Begin chase weaving by soaking two long pieces of space dyed #2 round reed. Put the ends behind two consecutive spokes and weave for several spokes, over and under, with the first weaver. Then weave over the same number of spokes in the alternate weaving path with the second weaver. See **DIAGRAM 3**. When the second weaver catches up with the first, drop it and again weave with the first one. Alternate the two weavers in this manner until the base measures approximately 8.5" diameter. Consult "Basket Class" for adding a new weaver and ending a weaver while chase weaving or twining.

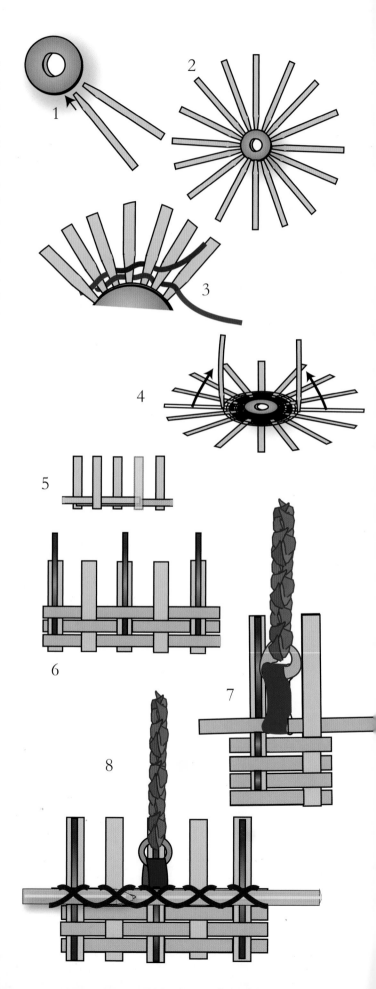

WEAVING THE SIDES OF THE BASKET:

Dampen the spokes at the edge of the weaving and upsett the spokes by bending them over on themselves to the inside of the basket. They won't stand permanently, but they will crease at the base and get the general idea of standing. See **DIAGRAM 4**.

Begin weaving with a soaked 3/8" weaver anywhere on the side of the basket and weave around in plain weave (over 1, under 1). End the weaver by weaving over the beginning to the 4th spoke and cutting. See **DIAGRAM 5**. After two or three rows, insert the space dyed overlays on either every spoke or every other spoke. See **DIAGRAM 6**. Weave 15 rows, starting and stopping each row at a different spot to avoid a buildup from overlapping the ends.

INSERTING HANDLE:

As you weave the 16th row, thread the weaver through the loop in the strap on two spokes that are on opposite sides of the basket. See **DIAGRAM 7**. With the strap in place on the outside of the basket, **DO NOT CUT THE** ends of the spokes. Place a piece of 3/8" flat oval reed around the top of the basket, covering the 16th row of weaving. Overlap the ends for 4" and shave them so the overlap is no thicker than a single thickness of 3/8" flat oval reed. Always make the overlapped end point in the direction you will be lashing.

Now place a piece of the 3/8" flat oval reed on the outside of the basket covering the same row and again pointing in the direction you will lash. Lash the rim in place with a long damp space dyed lasher. Lash in both directions for a double or X lashing. See **DIAGRAM 8** for lashed rim.

After the first (decorative) rim is in place, continue weaving seven more rows of plain weave in 3/8" flat reed. The last row will be a false rim and will be covered with the rim pieces.

SECOND RIM:

Dampen the tops of the spokes and bend the ones on the outside over the false rim to the inside. Tuck them behind the first available row of weaving on the inside. Cut the stakes on the inside flush with the top of the false rim. Position the two rim pieces of 3/8" flat oval reed just as you did before, one on the inside of the basket and one on the outside. Measure, allowing approximately 3"- 4" of overlap, and remove the rim pieces. Again, shave half the thickness from the top and the bottom of the ends so that the overlapped area is no thicker than a single thickness of flat oval reed. Replace the rim pieces, being sure that both overlaps are pointing in the direction you will lash. Place a piece of seagrass between the rim pieces this time as a filler. Start a long soaked lasher as described in "Basket Class" and lash through every space between the spokes. See **DIAGRAM 9** for lashing.

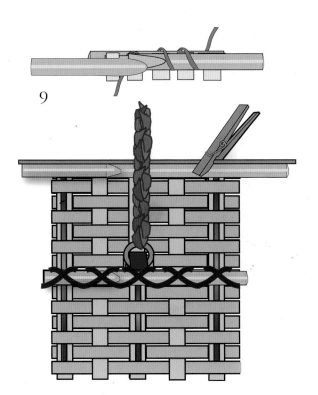

9

MAKING THE LID:

From the 5/8" flat reed, cut 16 pieces 8" long. Taper the ends as you did in the beginning of the base, and insert them into the slot in the "wooden donut ring," spacing them evenly.

With the wrong side up, begin two long space dyed #2 round weavers by just laying them anywhere on top of two consecutive spokes. Chase weave with both of them until the diameter of the lid is only slightly larger than the top of the basket. Refer to **DIAGRAM 3** for how to chase-weave. Cut pieces of 11/64" space dyed flat oval reed 2" long and insert them under the rows of weaving matching the placement of the pieces on the basket. Use **DIAGRAMS 5 & 6** for weaving.

Dampen and upsett the spokes, bending them over upon themselves. Weave four start-stop rows of plain weave with soaked 3/8" flat reed starting anywhere. Do not start and stop the rows at the same place. Then weave the fifth row with a piece of 7 mm as a false rim. Dampen and bend the ends of the spokes to the inside and push them under a row of weaving. Cut the ends so they do not show.

Referring back to **DIAGRAM 9,** place a soaked piece of 3/8" flat oval reed on the inside and the outside, overlapping the ends 2"-3" and shaving the top and bottom of the overlapped area so it isn't too thick. Make the ends point in the direction you will be lashing. Place the overlaps near, but not on top of each other. Begin lashing just past the overlaps. Place a piece of seagrass between the two rim pieces. Hold everything in place with clothespins. Start the lasher by taking it between the two rim pieces, over the wall of the lid, and down to the outside. Lash in every space. Then turn and lash in the other direction (double lash). End the lasher by the same means you began, cutting it so it doesn't show. Your knitting basket is complete. Say a little prayer of thanksgiving to the Abenaki and fill it with your new favorite (or old favorite) yarn. **HAPPY KNITTING !**

This "Old" Abenaki style ash knitting basket (used as the prototype) is in Lyn's collection

Amish Tray By Lyn Syler

When you see Lyn's Amish Tray you are immediately drawn to the beautiful colors and soft sheen of the dyed ash. Both colorways, the dark jewel tones of the Amish Tray and the rich southwest colors of Costa Mesa, showcase the talent Lyn brings to basketry and the magic of her color combinations. The technique used to weave the basket is basically the same as the quatrefoil. The pattern originally came from a Chitimacha tray made by Melissa Darden. It's an example of a very old technique simply made in contemporary colors.

Amish Colors

MATERIALS and PREPARATION

3/16" heavy ash (to be dyed for stakes and weavers)
Pine needles (rim)
¼" heavy ash (false rim)
Waxed linen and large tapestry needle (lashing)
Before dyeing, cut the 3/16" stakes - all 11" long

Dye the 11" stakes the following colors:
(Costa Mesa colors are in parentheses)
        14 fuchsia (pumpkin)
        18 teal (teal)
        16 purple (tan)
        20 black (blue)
Dye weavers black (teal)
Dye pine needles black (natural)

Dimensions: 6" x 6" x 2"
Shown in Costa Mesa Colors

NOTE FROM LYN:

You can use any number of pieces of any color, not necessarily the same that I have used. It's great in any combination of numbers or colors. Use as many different colors as you want and change them as often as you want. It's hard to make one that isn't nice.

This pattern is very logical. The secret is that the center of each side is either over or under 1,3,5 or 7 and everything else is over or under 4.

WEAVING THE BASE:

In this case, the base is the basket. Lay seven fuchsia pieces horizontally and weave one piece in vertically under the center piece. Weave in two more pieces (vertically) on either side of the first piece, going under the center three pieces.
See **DIAGRAM 1**.
Next weave in two more pieces vertically under the center five pieces.
Weave in two more pieces on each side UNDER all seven pieces for a total of seven vertically and horizontally.
See **DIAGRAM 2.**
At this point, notice that the last top and bottom pieces are woven under five and the last pieces on the other two sides are under seven. Number the sides as follows: top side (1), bottom side (3), right side (2), and left side (4). The rest of the directions will refer to these numbers. Also at this point, change to teal. Weave under all seven on sides 1 and 3. Weave over the center one and under the four on each side of it on sides 2 and 4. See **DIAGRAM 3.**
Weave the next pieces of teal over the center piece and under the rest on sides 1 and 3. On sides 2 and 4, weave over the center three and under four on each side. Weave the next four pieces as follows:
Sides 1 and 3: over center three, under the rest
Sides 2 and 4: over center five, under the rest
As you can see now, the pattern of the center weaving is 1,3,5,7 (either over or under) and everything else is 4's…either over or under.
The next piece on sides 1 and 3 will be over the center five, under four on both sides. On sides 2 and 4 it will be over seven and under four on both sides. See **DIAGRAM 4.**
Continue to add the pieces in this pattern until you have five teal pieces on sides 1 and 3, and four pieces on sides 2 and 4. The 5th piece on sides 2 and 4 will be woven under the center one and over four, under four on each side and is purple.
See DIAGRAM 5.
The next row around is:
Sides 1 & 3 under center one and over four, under four
Sides 2 & 4 under center three and over four, under four

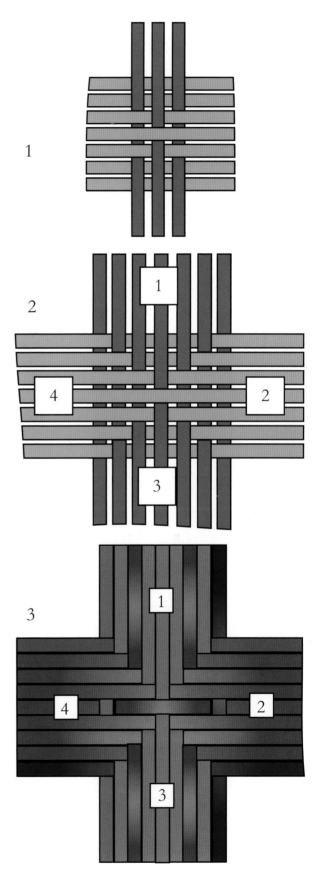

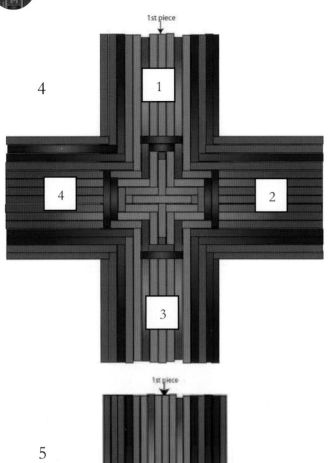

1st piece

4

1

2

3

4

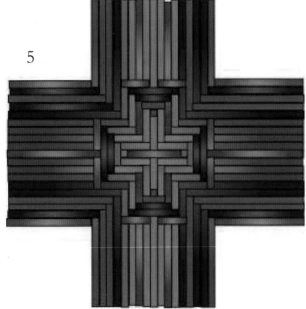

1st piece

5

Continue adding purple pieces in the pattern until there are four on all sides. Then change to black and put in five pieces on all four sides following the pattern.

WEAVING THE SIDES:

Locate a center of any side. The stroke on either side of the center is "over 4." Place the end of a long, dampened weaver so it is going over four stakes (starting on the second stake from the center) and moves the four over one stake to the right. Continue to weave under four, over four around the basket. Do not concern yourself with where the over fours fall after the beginning. See **DIAGRAM 6.** The over 4's move over one stake to the right every row. Weave six or seven "start-stop" rows. See "Basket Class" for detailed description of "start-stop" row. End each row by overlapping the ends to the 4th set of stakes.
See **DIAGRAM 7**.
Weave in a row of heavy ¼" ash for the false rim over two, under two. Pack all the rows very tightly down. Hold them in place with clothespins or alligator clips. Dampen the ends and bend one of the two over to the outside of the basket and push it behind a row or two of weaving. Cut the other end flush with the top of the false rim row.
 See **DIAGRAM 8.**

7

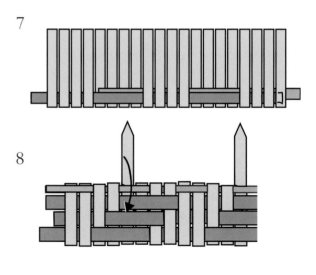

8

6

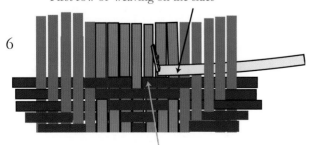

First row of weaving on the sides

Last row of weaving on the base

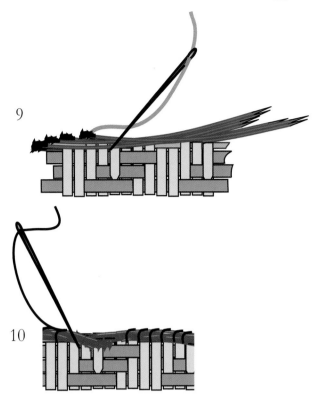

RIM THE BASKET:

To put on the rim, place 10-20 long pine needles on the rim, half on the inside and half on the outside. Thread the needle with waxed linen and tie it on to the rim to secure it. Lash around the rim going into every other space.
See **DIAGRAM 9.**

9

Keep a close eye on the inside of the basket as it is hard to see the needle coming out on the inside. Make sure the needle clears the pine needles. Stagger the ends of the pine needles so they don't run out at the same time. Add one every time an end is near. Place some of the ends on the left and some on the right. Cut some off early (or readjust them) just so you can add new ones, one at a time. Push the new end under the old ones, or let the new one rest on top. The tips of the needles can stay on or be cut later. If you need to, touch up the ends with black dye or magic marker. Take care to shape the corners of the tray while you are lashing the rim. End the pine needles by pushing the ends under the beginning. Back lash a few stakes (under the rim) to secure the end of the thread and cut as in **DIAGRAM 10.**

10

This tray, of course, was meant to hang so the base can be fully appreciated. If your intention was to make a great gift for someone else (or yourself), this it is. ENJOY!

"The Collection"
Created in Adobe Photoshop
by Carolyn Kemp

Arabian Nights By Debra Hammond

Dimensions for large 8" diameter x 5" high and small 4" diameter x 3.5" high

This beautifully designed basket is Debra Hammond's brainchild. It uses randing, Japanese weave, three and four-rod wale and a rolled border. Her addition of a wonderfully textured wool yarn adds yet another dimension....and the beads, another. It's fun to see the different patterns emerge when you change the color of weavers while doing a three or four-rod wale.

MATERIALS and PREPARATION
Note: Directions for "small" version are in( )

#4 (#1) round reed for spokes
#2 (#00) round reed for weavers, dye of your color choice
Heavy wool or wool blend yarn, preferably a large nubby type for weavers
Beads -32 beads in a size that will fit on #4 (#1) round reed
From #4 round reed, cut 16 spokes 36" long (#1 round reed, cut 16 spokes 20" long)

IMPORTANT: All weaving is done from the outside of the basket. Weaving should be packed down after every 2 or 3 rows. **Keep all weaving materials damp.**

WEAVING THE BASE:

Divide the spokes into four groups of four. Mark the centers of one from each group and use clothespins to hold each group together. Lay out base with spokes crossing at centers. The two bottom groups of four will form an X. Place the next group horizontally on top of the X and place the last group vertically on top of the horizontal group.

Begin weaving with a long flexible piece of #2 (#00) round reed. You will be looking at the outside of the basket as you weave. Start with the weaver on top of the top group of spokes, leaving a 12" tail. Then weave under one group, over one group, etc. After two rounds, pull both ends of the weaver to tighten. See **DIAGRAM 1.**

Then "back-weave" the 12" tail so it fills in the spaces between the groups of fours, actually creating an inner row of weaving. Back-weaving eliminates any holes or gaps between the groups of four. Debra's students are always amazed at how tight their weaving looks after doing this little trick ! See **DIAGRAM 2.**

End the tail on the back side beside the top vertical group of spokes, tuck the tail under the weavers and cut off. Resume weaving on the outside of the basket with the long weaver. Check to see that as you begin weaving (with the long weaver) that it is in position to go over the first group for the fourth time. Now weave over two spokes and under two spokes. See **DIAGRAM 3.** This will put the "overs" and "unders" in the alternate path ("overs" last row will now be "unders"). Continue weaving over four spokes, under four spokes for three rounds.

JAPANESE WEAVE:

At this point, begin weaving (JAPANESE weave) over two spokes,

1

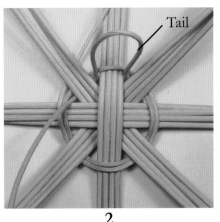

Tail

2

3

4

under one, continuously until the base is 4" (2") in diameter. See **DIAGRAM 4.**

"Dome" the base slightly with the center going away from you since you are weaving from the outside of the basket.

If your weaver runs out, tuck it down on the left side of the spoke after the spoke where it weaves behind. Tuck the end of the new weaver down on the right side of the spoke that the old weaver went behind. See **DIAGRAM 5.**

When your base is 4"(2") in diameter, stop weaving but DO NOT END THE WEAVER.

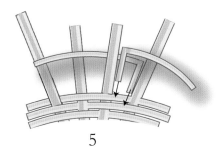

5

WEAVING THE SIDES:

Soak the spokes and crimp each spoke close to the weaving, gently bend them upward. See "Basket Class" for more instruction on crimping. See **DIAGRAM 6.**

6

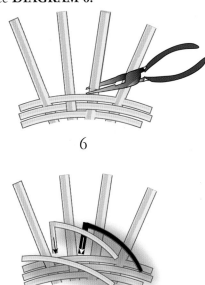

7

19

THREE ROD WALE:

If you have not done three and four rod wale refer to "Basket Class" for further explanation.

Now "add" two more #2 (#00) soaked weavers, one natural and one dyed. Insert one natural weaver on the right side of the next spoke to the right of where your original weaver comes out. Then, insert one dyed weaver on the right side of the next spoke.

See **DIAGRAM 7**

Hold the spokes up in a slightly flared position while weaving three-rod wale. Take the left weaver in front of two spokes, over the other two weavers, behind the next spoke and out. Repeat this sequence for 15 rows, letting the sides flare as you weave.

When one of your weavers runs out, tuck it down on the left side of the spoke after the spoke where it weaves behind. Tuck the end of the new weaver down on the right side of the spoke that the old weaver went behind.

Refer back to **DIAGRAM 5**.

After the first 15 rows, replace the left natural weaver with a dyed weaver. Weave 10 more rows of three-rod wale with one natural and two dyed weavers.

Replace the remaining weaver with a dyed weaver. Weave five more rows of three rod wale with three dyed weavers. This should be the widest point of the basket.

Next, replace the center dyed weaver with a wool weaver. Add a second piece of dyed #2 (#00) round reed under the first and third weavers. You now have two double #2 (#00) weavers and one of wool (see Detail Photo). Wet the spokes. At this point, decrease the diameter of the basket by pushing in on the spokes and putting more tension on the weavers. Weave eight rows of three-rod wale and end all weavers.

Soak the spokes and crimp them from front to back (inside of the basket to the outside) so as to encourage them to

8

Your Finished Basket!

Detail Photo

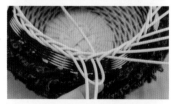

stand straight up. Place one bead on each spoke. You can use any size bead with a hole large enough to fit on the spoke.

FOUR ROD WALE:

For the top section of weaving, hold the spokes going straight up. Start by crimping the weavers about 1" from the end so they will be pointing upward and lie flat against the spokes. Using an alligator clip, clip the end of each weaver to the right side of four consecutive spokes. This way the ends will be caught up in the next few rows of your weaving. See **DIAGRAM 8**. Use one natural and three dyed weavers. Weave four rod wale by taking the left weaver in front of two spokes, behind two spokes and out. Repeat this sequence until your working weaver comes out in the last empty space.

At this point, weave a step-up by taking the right weaver in front of two spokes, behind two spokes and out. Repeat using each weaver one time, working in order from right to left. The "step-up" is completed. Weave a total of five rows of four-rod wale, ending each row with a step-up.

End weavers. Soak spokes and crimp, near the weaving, from side to side to prepare for making the border.

WEAVING THE ROLLED BORDER:

Row 1 - Take each spoke behind two spokes to the right and out
Row 2 - Take each spoke under two spokes to the right and into the basket
Row 3 - On the inside, take each spoke over two spokes to the right and down
Row 4 - Take each spoke over two spokes to right and down
Trim spoke ends on a slant when dry.

Finished Border

Ashley's Berry Basket Scarf

By Sherry Clayton Baldwin

The Basketweave Pattern (Barbara G. Walker's *A Treasury of Knitting Patterns*, 1968 by Charles Scribner's Sons, p.16-17) has long been a favorite of knitters and basketmakers. This version of the basketweave scarf is named for my precocious eleven-year-old knitting student, Ashley, who is constantly writing her own patterns and encouraging me to do so as well!

Dimensions: 52" long and 6" at the widest point - pictured with Dianne Kennedy's Abenaki Style Knitting Basket

MATERIALS

Two stitch markers
One yarn needle (for Kitchner stitch)
One row counter, if desired
Two skeins of Brown Sheep's COTTON FLEECE (53 colors)
      or a cone of COTTON FINE (using two strands held together)
Sample scarf is made with BERRY COTTON FLEECE (80% cotton, 20% wool)
      on size 5 needles

Needles: 16" or 24" circular or straight needles in size 5,
      or size that gives you a gauge you like
One size 6 needle, or one needle size larger than the size used
      to knit the scarf if you choose to finish with a
      three-needle bind-off

DIRECTIONS:

Cast on 34 stitches using the cable cast on method for maximum stretch. Refer to directions in your favorite "how-to knitting book" if you do not know how to cable cast on or see "Basket Class" for detailed description.

On the **FIRST** stitch of **EVERY** row, slip one stitch as if to purl (yarn in front).

Knit eight rows (garter stitch) remembering to slip the first stitch of every row as if to purl.

16 Row Basketweave Pattern Repeat: (Odd numbered rows are the right side)

Row 1: Slip one stitch as if to purl, knit 3, place marker. P3, ***K2, P4***,
    Repeat between * and * two more times; K2, P3, place second marker, K4

Row 2: Slip 1, K3, slide marker. K3, * **P2, K4** *. Repeat between * and * two more times.
    P2, K3, slide marker, K4

Row 3: Repeat Row 1

Row 4: Repeat Row 2

Row 5: Repeat Row 1

Row 6: Repeat Row 2

Row 7: Slip first stitch as if to purl, knit to end of row.

Row 8: Slip 1, K3, P26, K4

Row 9: Slip 1, K3, ***K2, P4** *. Repeat between * and * three more times; K2, K4

Row 10: Slip 1, K3, * **P2, K4** *. Repeat between * and * three more times; P2, K4

Row 11: Repeat Row 9

Row 12: Repeat Row 10

Row 13: Repeat Row 9

Row 14: Repeat Row 10

Row 15: Repeat Row 7

Row 16: Repeat Row 8

Two Halves Joined
with Three Needle Bind Off

Repeat this 16–row pattern six times (or the number of times to achieve the length of pattern panel you want). You are now ready to work on the right side of the scarf. This row sets up the ribbed (neck portion of the scarf). Slip the first stitch as if to purl, work in K2, P2 ribbing to the last stitch, K1.

Repeat this row 99 more times, or until the neck length is one-half the length you desire it to be. Do not cut the yarn until you choose your seam finishing method.

Put these stitches on a spare needle (#5 is best) and make the second half of the scarf exactly the same way as the first, using the second skein of yarn. DO NOT CUT YARN.

When the second half of the scarf is completed, you are ready to do the three-needle bind-off or Kitchner stitch to join the two halves. Be sure to bind off loosely so the seam join does not ruin the look of the scarf. For the more experienced knitter, you can knit the entire neck length by reversing the 16-row pattern repeats thus avoiding any seam or join.

Find directions for Kitchner stitch or three-needle bind-off in your favorite knitting book and join the two halves of the scarf. The most invisible join is the Kitchner and the strongest seam is the three-needle bind-off.

Cut the yarn from both skeins and weave in the ends.

Carry your favorite basket when you wear your new BASKETWEAVE SCARF!

Beginner Market Basket

By Lyn Syler

This beginner market basket is a great "first basket" but worthy of making again and again. It starts with a square base and goes up to a rounded top, simplifying the shaping process. The basket truly weaves itself. Have fun doing your first project with Lyn's detailed instructions and your own touch of creativity.

NOTE: Use general directions for all sizes. Use the following sizes of reed and measurements for the 10" and 8" sizes.

10" Basket:

To make the 10" basket, cut 14 pieces 26" long from 3/4" flat reed. Weave with either 1/2" or 5/8" flat reed. The base should be approximately 7" square (7 pieces x 7 pieces) Use a 10" notched handle.

8" Basket:

To make the 8" basket, use either 10 pieces of 1" cut 22", lay out the base (5 pieces x 5 pieces) or 14 pieces of 5/8" also cut 22" for stakes, lay out base (7 pieces x 7 pieces).

Weave with 1/2" or 3/8" flat reed. The base should be approximately 6" square. NOTE: Sometimes the base measurement may be different. One of mine actually measures closer to 7" x 7", and the sides go almost straight up. If the base measures 6" x 6", the basket will need to flare to 8" for the handle to fit. Use an 8" notched handle.

Dimensions: 9" x 9" base x 12" high
including handle

MATERIALS and PREPARATION

1" flat reed (stakes) - cut 14 pieces each 31" long and mark centers on each piece
5/8" flat reed (weavers)
1/2" flat reed (false weaver)
5/8" flat oval (rim)
1/4" flat reed (lashing)
Seagrass (rim filler)
Large notch handle (approximately 24" from notch to notch)
Dye : Colors used for pictured basket - Rit brand; Denim Blue, Scarlet Red & Dark Green
　　　(for space dyed weavers and stakes) or you can leave your reed "natural" (undyed)
　　　as a nice alternative to space dyed
Note: All reed must be soaked for a few minutes until it is pliable
The flat oval reed is thicker and will therefore require a longer soaking time to become workable

CUTTING THE REED & WEAVING THE BASE:

Cut 14 pieces of 1" flat reed, each 31" long. With a pencil, mark the centers of two pieces with an "X" on the wrong side. (The wrong side of the flat reed is the rough side). Soak all 14 pieces of reed for 1-2 minutes in cool water. Place 7 of the wet pieces (stakes) horizontally (wrong side up) , about 3/8" apart. Be sure the fourth or middle strip has its center marked. Once these 7 are in place, weave the other marked stake perpendicularly, over and under. Match the two center marks. See **DIAGRAM 1.** Using a heavy book or **spoke weight** will hold the stakes in place while you continue to work. Now, weave the other six stakes over and under, three on each side of the middle stake, being certain the weaving alternates on each row. You have now formed the bottom of the basket. With a tape measure or yardstick, measure from side to side at several points to be sure the bottom is square. It should be 9" square. See **DIAGRAM 2.**

UPSETTING THE SIDES:

To "upsett" the sides of the basket or to make the stakes stand upright, you must bend and press each stake all the way over on itself to form a permanent crease at the bottom of the stake. You may want to use a flat ruler, and press the stakes over the ruler in the direction of the woven bottom.
See **DIAGRAM 3.** The stakes will return themselves to an approximately upright position, but the sides will not stay perfectly upright until several rows of weaving have been completed around the basket.

WEAVING THE SIDES OF THE BASKET:

Soak one long strip of 5/8" flat reed (weaver) for 1-2 minutes. Notice on the bottom of the base some stakes originate under the weaving and some originate from the top. Begin weaving (with the wet weaver) by placing the end on the outside of one of the stakes that originates from the bottom of the weaving. See **DIAGRAM 4.**

Weave with the right side of the reed on the outside of the basket. This way, you are making the bottom stakes stand upright first. The next row of weaving will pick up the other stakes. This basket has a square base but a rounded top; you do not need to "square" the corners, just "round" them as you weave.

When you have woven all the way around the basket, allow enough reed to overlap the starting point and then cut the weaver behind the 4th stake. This is called a "start/stop" row; refer to "Basket Class" for details. See **DIAGRAM 5.**

Re-wet weavers or stakes that become dry. Begin weaving the next row, and each row thereafter, in a different place so as not to get a buildup from starting and stopping at the same place. Continue weaving in this manner, pushing each completed row down snugly against the previous row, for a total of eleven rows. Last, weave a false weaver (a row of 1/2" flat reed). This row is covered by the rim and should always be narrower than the rim material.

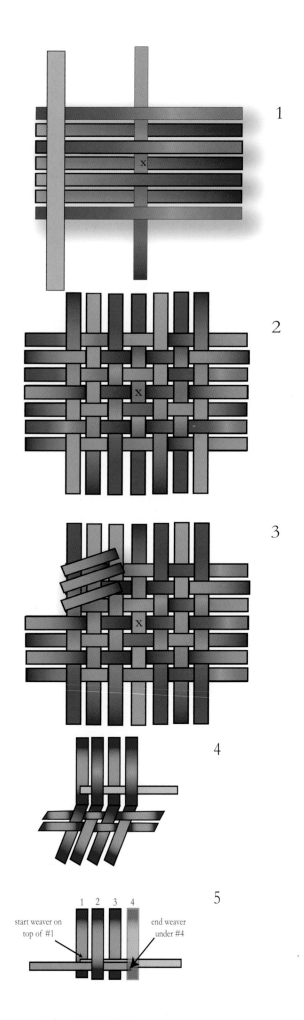

1

2

3

4

5

start weaver on
top of #1

end weaver
under #4

1 2 3 4

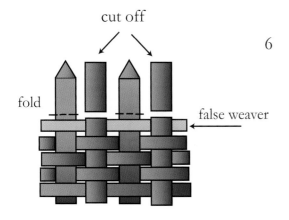

cut off

fold

false weaver

6

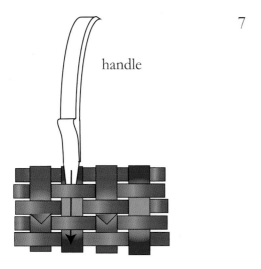

handle

7

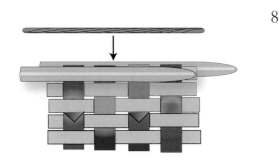

8

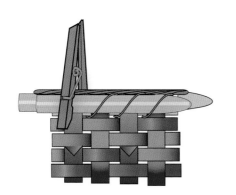

9

(lashing is only shown on one
direction, reverse to X)

FINISHING THE TOPS OF THE STAKES & INSERTING THE HANDLE:

When you have finished weaving, you will find that half your stakes are behind the false weaver and half are in front. Wet the top part of the stakes again. With scissors or reed cutters, cut the **inside** stakes so they are even with the last row of weaving. Then, with scissors or reed cutters, cut the outside stakes to a point. Bend the pointed stakes over and insert them into the weaving inside the basket. Be sure the end is hidden behind a weaver. See **DIAGRAM 6.** At this point, insert the handle, as in **DIAGRAM 7,** on the inside of the basket with the center stakes across from each other that are cut off. Align the notch with the bottom of the top row of weaving. The rim will "sit" on the "notch" and prevent the handle from pulling out.

APPLYING THE RIM:

With all the outside stakes pushed down into the weaving and the handle in place, wrap a piece of soaked 5/8" flat oval reed around the inside top edge of the basket, covering only the top row of weaving. Overlap the ends about 3" and cut. Shave some of the thickness from the overlapped area so it is no thicker than a single thickness. Hold the reed in place with clothespins. Then place a second piece around the outside, covering only the top row of weaving again. Hold both pieces in place with the same clothespins. Overlap the ends and shave them as before. Position the 2 overlapped areas near but not on top of each other. Lastly, lay a piece of seagrass between the 2 rim pieces allowing the ends to overlap 1" to 1 1/2".
See **DIAGRAM 8.**

LASHING THE RIM:

With a long soaked piece of 1/4" flat reed, begin to lash all the rim pieces together as in **DIAGRAM 9.** If necessary, use an awl to open the space for the lasher under the rim, between the stakes. Lose the ends of the lasher between the rim pieces so that the lasher does not pull out.
The lasher goes up under the inside rim (wrong side up), over the wall of the basket, down to the outside under the outside rim. Leave a "tail" sticking out from under the rim. It can be trimmed later.
If you need additional instructions on doing the rim, refer to "Basket Class."

Beginner Pine Needle Project

By Dory Maier and Dianne Masi

Dimensions: 2" high x 3 1/2" diameter

This basket is a starting place for your creativity as pine needles can be coiled around any object that has holes; a sea shell that has been drilled, a walnut slice, a piece of pottery or ceramic or a weathered circle of driftwood. The possibilities are endless. The size and shape are dependent on the number of rows added to the basic directions we are providing. One of the really neat things about coiling is the way a basket can change in design as you weave.

MATERIALS and PREPARATION

1 oz. pine needles
10' Artificial sinew
Size 16 embroidery needle
Walnut slice
Gauge: 1 ½" piece of sipping straw

Preparation of needles:
The pine needles are prepared by removing sheaths, washing needles in warm soapy water, rinsing well in cool water and wrapping them in a towel to absorb the excess water. Needles can be used damp or dry.

Preparation of sinew:
Divide the sinew into 5 pieces much the same way that one divides embroidery floss.

LET'S GET STARTED:

1. Knot the sinew into any hole.
2. Take ten pine needles and hold them in your left hand with pointed ends to the left.
3. Place the bundle of needles on top of the nut slice, over your knot with the sinew in front.
    See **DIAGRAM 1.**
4. Over cast the bundle and come back through the same hole. Pull tightly.
5. Over cast the bundle front to back and pull the sewing needle through the back side of the next hole to the left
6. Over cast the bundle front to back and come back through the same hole. Over cast to the left and into the back side of the next hole. Continue around through all the holes. When you come to where the blunt ends are in your way, hold them down with a new bundle laid on top of the blunt ends. Try to hide them as much as you can. This is messy and the toughest part of starting. Each stitch has two parts. First, over cast over the coil (bundle), coming out in the same hole in which you started. This makes the bar; a perpendicular stitch. Second, over cast around the pine needle coil and come through the next left hand hole in the base from wrong side to right side of the walnut slice.

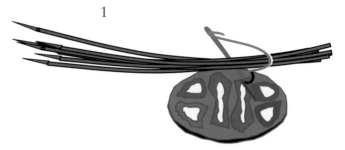

7. This makes a slanted stitch to the left. Together the two parts are called "The Wheat Stitch".
    See **DIAGRAMS 2 & 3.**

Note: After a couple of stitches, put the gauge over the needles and add pine needles every few stitches. See DIAGRAM 2. Keep the gauge full. The pine needles should be tight in the gauge but not so tight that the gauge will not turn easily.

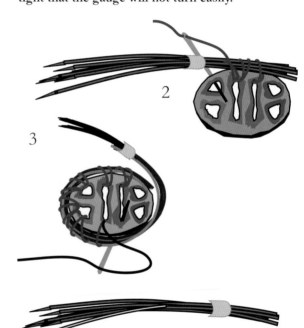

Adding Needles to Gauge

8. As you start the next row, insert your sewing needle (from the back of your work) at a slight angle, just to the right of the bar stitch in the coil beneath and pull it out just to the left of the stitch, picking up about 1/3 of the coil as you do so. Keep the new coil directly on top of the one beneath.
    See **DIAGRAM 4.**
9. Continue making the wheat stitch around the nut slice in every stitch on this row only. After the second row, you will only be inserting the needle in the first part of the wheat stitch (or bar part of the stitch) until you have a diameter of about three inches. Then stop when you are opposite your starting point on the nut slice.

ENDING AND ADDING THREAD:

When the thread gets to be about 3-4 inches long, use the sewing needle to make a knot in the top of the last stitch and then poke the needle down through the top of the last row. Bring it out several rows below or to the side, and cut it off. To add a new thread, insert the needle several rows below, or to the side, leaving a tail, and bring the needle out in the top of the last stitch made. Then continue. Cut tails off.

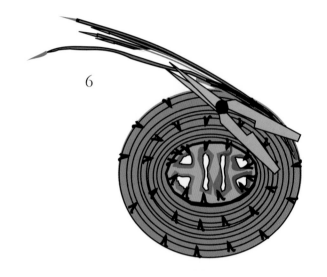

6

10. You are now going to start the sides. Lay the working round down on the table and pull the coil up and place it on top of the last row. Insert the needle from the back to front at a 45 degree angle from right to left, and coming out about 1/2 way up through the row that is on the table. See **DIAGRAM 5.** Finish the wheat stitch and continue up for about two inches.

11. As you get closer to two inches in height, remove the gauge and stop adding needles. Cut the longest needles back randomly as in **DIAGRAM 6.** As the bundle gets smaller, work the last two or three stitches right over the stitches in the row below. Finish off the sinew by pushing the needle back through the work.

Congratulations, you have completed your Pine Needle Project!

Profile of basket

Boutique Tissue
by Patti Quinn Hill

"Utilitarian baskets are not my usual forte, but I had the desire to create something that was functional as well as artistic. The tissue basket was one I could use myself, so that is how this little gem was created. Since the box itself is not part of the basket, you get to see the inside, and the tissues still pop up the same way."
Patti

MATERIALS and PREPARATION

1 full sheet - 140 lb. Arches rough watercolor paper 20"x 30" cut to below lenghts after painting
  Rims- 2 @ 30" – ¾" wide each, using 1 ½" of paper
  Uprights – 22 @ 15" – ¼" wide each, using 4" of paper
  Weavers – 20 @ 30" – ¼" wide each, using 6" of paper
Acrylic paints - Patti used turquoise, bronze, copper and gold metallic
Hand-cranked pasta cutter (optional - substitute carving knife and straight edge) to cut paper
Ruler
Scissors, pushpins, #18 tapestry needle
4 ½ yards of waxed linen or other thick thread
White glue
Acrylic varnish
Mold – see dimensions below **or** use boutique tissue box (leaving tissues inside for firmness)
Small clips

BASKET MOLD: Top: 4 3/8" x 4 3/8" Bottom: 4 1/4" x 4 1/4" Height: 4 3/4"
The mold is square. The square top of the mold is slightly larger than the square bottom of the mold so the sides are tapered from the top down to the bottom. The best wood to use is white pine. Or you can use house insulation with plastic wallpaper corner covers to keep the sides from rounding off as you weave.

PAINTING THE PAPER: "Cut your paper in half the long way. Before you start to paint your paper, try to visualize the inside and outside of your basket. You have 4 surfaces that need to be painted. Two surfaces will become the outside of your basket and the other two surfaces will become the inside of your basket. Therefore, one piece of paper will be painted on one side to become your outside uprights and painted on the other side to become your inside uprights. The other piece of paper will be painted on both sides to become your weavers. You can determine later which of these papers you would like to use for the curls. The paper that I painted for the basket in the photograph was all done with a sponge. See **DIAGRAM 1.** First, I sprayed the paper with water, then dipped the sponge into the bronze paint and used a scrubbing motion to apply the paint. Then I used a dabbing method to sponge layers of paint in copper, gold, and bronze metallic colors on top. The same technique was used to paint the turquoise color."

1

Decide what painted paper you want to use for your rims. True up the edge of the paper. Cut two ¾" wide pieces 30" long for rims using scissors or a carving knife. If you do not have a pasta cutter, cut all the uprights and weavers using a straight edge and carving knife.

USING FETTUCCINI CUTTER:

The fettuccini part of the pasta cutter will cut your strips ¼" wide. Attach the pasta cutter to the corner of a table so that when your paper comes down, it will go past the table edge. When using the pasta cutter, position your paper in the center of the blades, dividing the waste on the edges evenly. Try to keep your paper going straight so that you will have as many whole pieces as possible. If your paper gets crooked, you will lose whole pieces on both edges. When you start turning the handle, only crank a couple of turns at a time making sure that the paper does not curl back up into the pasta cutter. You will need to look under the pasta cutter and keep straightening out the paper until it falls past the table edge. See **DIAGRAM 2.**

2

Insert 4" of paper (paper's full length-30") for uprights through pasta cutter. This will give you some extra. From this cut 22 pieces @ 15" long each (cut 11 pieces in half). It will take 6" of paper for weavers. But the pasta cutter is not that wide, so you will have to insert your paper in two batches through the pasta cutter. This will give some extra. Leave the weavers their full length (30"). It takes about 20 weavers to weave the basket.

Whatever pieces you have left keep whole, because you may want to use these for curls.

LAY OUT THE BASE:

1. Take two uprights and put a light pencil mark in the center of each one. Cross these two pieces perpendicular at the marks. These will be your center uprights. Keep track of the center.

2. Weave two uprights on all sides of these center pieces for a total of ten uprights, five going in each direction. Have the negative spaces between the uprights be about 1/8" and make sure the ends of the uprights line up.

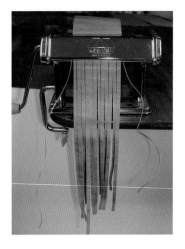

3

3. Add three more uprights on the top and bottom horizontally while making sure the ends are lined up. After all 11 uprights are woven in horizontally and five are woven in vertically, place the base on the bottom of the mold or tissue box as in **DIAGRAM 3**, to see if the 11 uprights fit. Do any adjusting necessary of the 11 uprights at this time. It is easier to adjust these 11 horizontally when there are only five going vertically. Secure this good measurement with clips.

4. Add three uprights on each side of the center vertically, giving you 11 woven in each direction. Place the basket base on the bottom of the mold and make adjustments to fit exactly all the way around. Make sure all negative spaces are even squares.

5. Decide which side is going to be the outside of your basket. Have the inside of the basket facing up and upsett all of the uprights. This means put a sharp crease by folding the uprights along the edges of the woven base. See **DIAGRAM 4.**

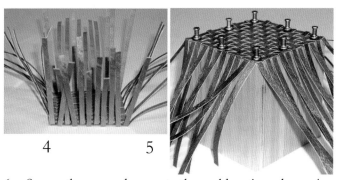

4   5

6. Secure the woven base onto the mold or tissue box using push-pins. See **DIAGRAM 5**. Place the push-pins in the negative spaces around the edge of the base (do not pierce the paper). Cushion between the basket and the push-pins with a scrap piece of paper or felt so that the push-pin does not mark the basket.

WEAVING UP THE SIDES:

1. Start the weaver on an upright that originates from underneath the base, going over one under one. See **DIAGRAM 6.** Weave snugly all the way around the mold and when you get back to where you started, overlap your weaver for four uprights ending where the weaver is hidden behind an under. Cut the weaver flush with the edge of that upright so that it is hidden. Never do overlaps around a corner.

6

2. Start each new row the same way on a different side of the basket. After you weave in three rows, make sure all rows are packed tightly and next to the base. There should be no spaces between the rows.

3. Always start each new row on an over and end it overlapping four uprights, stopping on an under.
   Keep each row packed tightly to the row below with no space between rows. Make sure uprights are staying evenly spaced. **Do not weave tightly around the mold.** Just weave next to it; otherwise, the basket may be hard to remove.

CURLS (optional):

There are unlimited curl design possibilities. How many strips you will need will be determined by how many curls you place on your basket. Curls can be placed covering each row as your weave or can be added at the end when the basket is completed.

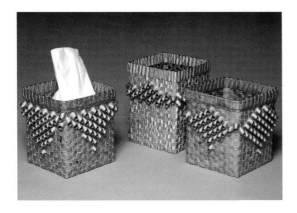

1. Start your curl piece on an under and put on a clip to secure it. Wrap the piece completely around clockwise if you are right handed and counterclockwise if you are left handed making a small circle and then place the piece behind the next under. See **DIAGRAM 7.**
   Do this same technique, making curls wherever you want them to appear. In other words, all of the curls are done on an over and then secured behind an under.

7

2. You may need to splice a piece in to complete the row of curls. Splice on an under overlapping the pieces making a double thickness. Clip the splice to hold it securely until you get the next row of weaving in above it.

3. When you get to the end of the row of curls, cut and hide the end of the piece behind the under where you started. This will make a double thickness here.

REMOVE FROM MOLD:

1. Twist the push-pins while removing from mold and then pull the basket off the mold.

2. All uprights on the inside of the basket are folded over to the outside and then cut just above the bottom of the last row of weaving. Using white glue, glue these folded ones down to the last row of weaving and clip to dry. Cut all of the uprights that are on the outside of the basket flush with the top of the last row of weaving. See **DIAGRAM 8.**

8

9

10

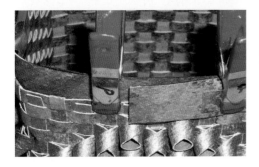

11

ATTACHING THE RIM:

1. Take one of the ¾" pieces that will be for the inside rim and cut off the corners, making the piece have a flat point on the end. Place this point on the inside of the basket at the right corner and clip it on the basket making sure that it does not go below the last row of weaving. See **DIAGRAM 9.** Clip snugly all the way around the basket. When you get to where you started, the end goes behind the beginning for about 2".

   As in **DIAGRAM 10,** place the end behind the starting point so that you have a nice smooth overlap without a break in the middle and your flat point is showing in the corner.

2. Start the outside rim on the same side of the basket as you started the inside rim. Place it half way over just where your inside overlap ended. Clip snugly all the way around, flush with bottom of last row of weaving.

3. When you get back to where you started, overlap to the right corner of that side and put a flat point on the piece. So, both of the overlaps are on the same side of the basket. See **DIAGRAM 11.** This is so that you will have room for adjustment at the end of the lashing. You can lash a lot tighter than the clips will hold the rim.

LASHING:

1. Thread the needle with the 4 ½ yards of lashing thread to do double lashing. This amount is just enough if you will lash very tightly (add more if you are concerned). Start the lashing to the right of all of the overlaps. Take the long end tail of the

thread and insert it going upward between the inside of the basket and the inside rim. Do this at the space between the second and third uprights to the right of the outside rim overlap. Pull it up and over the top of the basket and insert it between the outside of the basket and the outside rim. Leave a 4" tail hanging down on the outside of the basket.
See **DIAGRAM 12.**

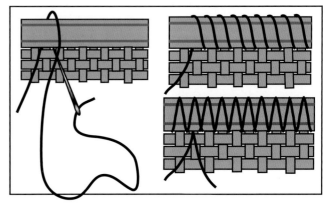

12

2. When you get to where you started your lashing and all spaces between the uprights have been filled, turn back and go the other way making "V's" on the rim with the thread. This is called double lashing. Go all the way around and through each space and back to where the lashing originally started.

3. After you have put the needle in the last space and pulled the thread inside the basket, and there are "V's" above every upright, it is time to tie it off. Place the needle going upward between the inside rim and the inside of the basket, pull it up and over the top of the basket and then insert the needle going down between the outside rim and outside of the basket, pulling snugly. Tie a square knot and cut the tails and push the knot up under the rim.

FINISHING
1. Brush the basket with an acrylic varnish to make it stiff. Cut the varnish 2 parts varnish to 1 part water. Or use an acrylic spray varnish.
2. When the basket dries, take the tissue out of the box and place it in the basket just like it was in the box. The tissues will still pop up.

Braided & Twill Tote

by Eileen LaPorte

MATERIALS and PREPARATION

3/8" flat oval or 7mm flat oval (for weavers and spokes) - cut 21 spokes at 26" and 11 spokes at 32"
    Please note that if you use the 7mm flat oval as weavers, you will need to weave a few more rows to compensate for the smaller size
    Mark each 26" spoke on the flat side, 10" from one end. Mark the 32" spokes 10" from one end
11/64" or 3/16" flat oval - for braid weave
3/8" flat - 40" for rim row
1/2" flat oval - inside & outside rims
Common Cane - several long pieces - for lashing the base
Waxed linen - 4 yards of 3 or 4 ply for lashing the rim
Seagrass - about 40" for rim filler
23" square notched handle with grip and 11"-12" spread - sand the handle smooth to the touch and taper and thin the ends to a gradual point
Macrame board or any board at least 10" wide for holding base
2 rubber bands- place the 2 rubber bands about 1"- 2" apart on the board about 5" from the bottom of the board
Place all 21 of the 26" spokes vertically on your board under the two rubber bands
    The 10" marks will be just above the rubber bands at the bottom of the board
Do not worry about the spacing just yet

THE BASE:

Begin with the marked 32" spoke. Place it horizontally on top of the 21 spokes just above the marks. The 10" mark on the 32" spoke will be just left of the 1st spoke on the left. The spokes will all be lashed rather than woven together. The base should be lashed tightly with only enough space between spokes to accommodate the cane.
See **DIAGRAM 1.** (Not all 21 spokes are shown in diagram). Start lashing on the left with the shiny cane side up facing you.
You need a piece of cane about 36" long to go all the way across the width of the base; it distracts from the pattern to start a new lasher in the middle.
Tuck a 3" - 4" tail under the rubber bands for now. Take the long end of the cane straight up and over the 32" horizontal spoke and wrap it behind the first vertical spoke, coming out on the right side of this spoke and under the horizontal spoke.
See **DIAGRAM 2.**
Now lash onto the second vertical spoke in the same manner. Wrap the cane up and over the horizontal spoke, behind the second vertical spoke, and come out on the bottom side of the horizontal spoke. Continue until you have lashed the first horizontal spoke on to all 21 vertical spokes. Lash left to right. **DIAGRAM 3** shows the first five vertical spokes lashed onto the horizontal spoke.

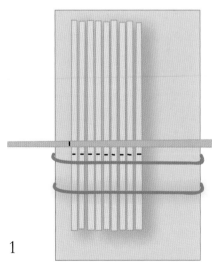

1

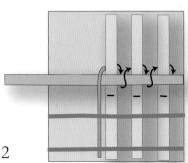

2

33

Dimensions: 10" long x 7 1/2" wide and 6 1/2" high (not including handle)

Eileen developed this basket several years after writing the "German Tribute" pattern. Her students loved the lashed base and the beauty of the unique Braid Weave; however, she stopped teaching it because the original handle became harder and harder to obtain. But basketmakers kept asking Eileen to teach the pattern. Finally, she was directed to a new handle. She made a few necessary adjustments to the pattern, and the result is this wonderful Braided and Twill Tote. Thanks to those folks who kept hounding Eileen to bring this pattern to us.

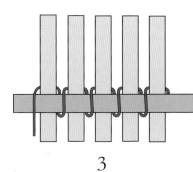

3

Note: This is a tight weave and nearly impossible to readjust without taking the lashing apart. Therefore, at this point check to see if your base measures 10" along the horizontal spoke. If you find that your base is not 10", take out the lashing and change the spacing between the vertical spokes to correct the final measurement. The base length is very important because the handle is a fixed dimension and has very little flexibility. If your base is too long or too short, the handle will not fit. Take your time as you lash the base, and later weave the sides, to check your dimensions with this fact in mind.

Place the second horizontal spoke above the first and take the cane and bring it over the two horizontal spokes, leaving a cane width space in between the spokes. Lash this spoke on by going to the left. Go behind the vertical spoke from the top right and back up under the second horizontal spoke in between the first and second vertical spokes. You will continue lashing on the second horizontal spoke in this manner. Right to left. See **DIAGRAM 4.**

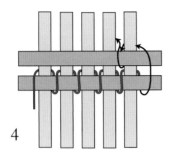

4

Hint: If the cane will not go all the way across the base, start a new lasher leaving a tail as you did in the very beginning. It is easier to tuck the old and new lasher after the base is finished.

Continue lashing the base until all eleven horizontal spokes are lashed on. Now go back to any place where you left tails and make a simple knot and leave a tail. The tail will be caught in the side weaving for about two rows and then cut off. Remove the base from the board.

THE SIDES:

Wet the base of the spokes and sharply upsett the sides. Taper a piece of soaked 3/8" flat oval for about 6".
Do a continuous weave with Japanese weave - over 2 and under 1 for a total of five rows. The last row will be tapered to match the beginning taper so that the two will equal the width of one weaver.

See **DIAGRAM 5.**

5

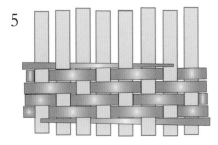

KEEP THE SIDES OF
YOUR BASKET
PERPENDICULAR TO
THE BASE. KEEP THE
SPACE BETWEEN THE
SPOKES AT 11/64".

BRAID WEAVE:

Now you will weave a 3" section in a continuous braid weave with three pieces of wet 11/64" flat oval. Because you will be weaving with three weavers, I strongly recommend that you do not use long pieces (pieces should each be about 6'-8' long). Taper one end of each piece for about 6".

Place the three weavers (A, B & C) behind the first three spokes (1,2,& 3) on the left of the long side. As in **DIAGRAM 6**, take the first weaver (A) and go in front of the next two spokes (2 & 3) and at the same time go under the third weaver (C) and then behind the next spoke (4) and out. You will now take the next weaver (B) and go in front of the next two spokes (3 & 4) and at the same time go under the weaver that is on the top (C). Think of the two weavers on the right forming a V on its side. You will take the weaver (C) on the left and go in front of the two spokes (4 & 5) on the right and split the V (IT IS GOING UNDER THE TOP WEAVER) and go behind the next spoke. I learned this trick from Flo Hoppe's book, *Wicker Basketry*. Be sure to keep your weaving tight and each row packed as you go. It is very difficult to pack when you reach the top.
See **DIAGRAM 6.**

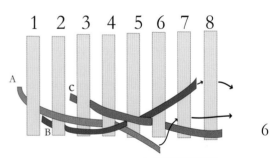

6

From now on, you will pick up the farthest LEFT weaver every stroke, go over the next two spokes and under the next while going under the top weaver, always coming out to the front.

You can see if you have made a mistake by checking the inside of your basket. The weavers will alternately be slanting up or down on each spoke, and each spoke should have the slants going only in one direction. If the weavers slant up and down on the same spoke, you have made a mistake. Check the inside of your basket often.

ADDING A NEW WEAVER:

When you have about 3" of weaver left it is time to add on a new weaver. Place the new weaver on top of the old weaver and hide the beginning when you go behind a spoke. Weave with the double weaver for a couple of spokes. Trim the old weaver after you have woven over and under at least four spokes. You may need to shave down the weavers if they are too thick when doubled. See "Basket Class" for details on adding a weaver.

Weave the braid weave until this section measures 3". End your weaving by tapering the last weaver about 6" to match the beginning weaver.

Now you will go back to the Japanese weaving with the 3/8" flat oval for a total of 4 rows. Don't forget to taper the beginning and ending weavers just as you did before.

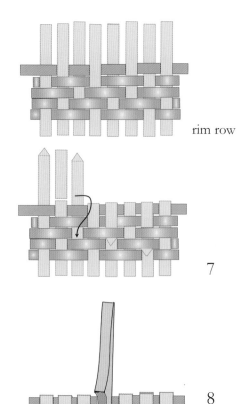

rim row

7

RIM ROW:

Weave one row of start/stop weaving of over 1 and under 1 with a wet piece of 3/8" flat. Dampen all the outside spokes and tuck them into the weaving inside the basket for 2-3 rows. Cut off the remaining spokes flush with the top edge. See **DIAGRAM 7.**

8

HANDLE:

Line up the notch of the handle with the rim row and check to see where to insert the tip of the handle. It just needs to be inserted into a couple of rows of weaving.
See **DIAGRAM 8.**

RIM:

Measure around the top of the basket allowing for about a 3" overlap for both the inside and outside rim. Fasten the rim on with clothespins or cable ties with the seagrass filler between the inside and outside rims.
See **DIAGRAM 9.**

Thread the waxed linen with the tapestry needle. Leave a tail of the waxed linen and lash the rim. When you get all the way around the rim, you will have both ends of the waxed linen to the inside of the basket. Tie a square knot, then thread the ends up between the rim and the basket to hide them.

Inserted Handle and Lashed Rim

9

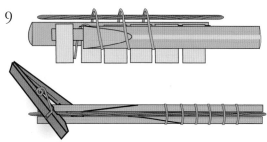

Confetti Twill

By Lyn Syler

Many of our baskets are based on creations of Sosse Baker. This cat head basket, utilizing continuous weave, is one of them. We owe her a huge debt of gratitude. Have fun with the colors and their placement. The sky is the limit! This is a good opportunity to just have fun with colors and shape. It's hard to make one that isn't great!

Dimensions: 4" x 4" base x 7" high plus handle

MATERIALS and PREPARATION

7mm flat oval reed (stakes)
11/64" flat oval reed (weavers)
½" flat oval reed (rim)
3/8" flat reed (false rim)
6"- 8" swing handle
Lyn's Indian Swing Handle made by Poplin Hollow Baskets 536 Poplin Hollow Rd. Linden, TN 37096
(931) 589-5126   email: poplinhollow@hotmail.com

Dye approximately ½ hank of 7mm flat oval reed in 5 or 6 different colors for stakes

NOTE: To do a continuous o2, u1 weave around any basket, the total number of stakes must be divisible by 3 (the total stakes in the stroke), plus or minus 1.
Example: This basket is 13 stakes x 13 stakes, a total of 52 stakes, which, when divided by 3, is 17 plus 1.

WEAVING THE BASE:

From the different colors, cut 26 pieces in various colors. As you lay out the base, keep in mind how they will look standing up on the sides, i.e., reds on the corners will be side by side when they stand.

The base is woven in a 2/2 twill. Mark the centers of all the pieces on the right side. Lay 13 pieces horizontally, aligning center marks. Weave the first piece in on the center marks, from bottom up: o2, u2, o2, u2, o2, u2, o1.
Row 2: u1, o2, u2, o2, u2, o2, u2
Row 3: u2, o2, u2, o2, u2, o2, u1
Row 4: o1, u2, u2, o2, u2, o2, u2
These four rows are repeated to the right for three rows and to the left for six rows. The base should resemble **DIAGRAM 1.** True the base to approximately 4" x 4".

FORMING THE CAT-HEAD BASE:

Taper one end of a long soaked weaver for long enough to go around one revolution. Make it at least half its normal width. See "Basket Class" for tapering a weaver.
With the base flat on a table, right side up, weave around the base, over 2, under 2, (a locking row) for one row only. Weave opposite the base weaving to lock. See "Basket Class" for detailed instructions on locking row. See **DIAGRAM 2.**
On the second row, begin the pattern stroke, over 2, under 1. Now begin to "sunburst" the stakes (push the stakes from the center of the sides to the corner). See **DIAGRAM 3.** Eventually fill in the corner spaces with stakes.

Now pinch the corner stakes together and lift up on the corners as you weave around. As you are holding the corners up and together, pull firmly on the weaver to keep the stakes in place. See **DIAGRAM 4** for this technique.
If the "feet" (or "ears") aren't pronounced enough for you, place your thumbs in the corners (from the inside) and push the corners out. See Photo Detail for finished feet.
Resume weaving until you have woven eight or nine rows. Add weavers as needed by hiding the end of a new wet weaver behind a stake and weaving with the two until the old one runs out. Cut the end of the old piece so it doesn't show from the inside. When there are approximately nine rows, lift the basket from the table and hold it with the ends of the stakes pointing away from you. Just lifting the base will cause the sides to begin to point upward. You must determine just how much you want them to stand and control the shape. If the sides are going in too fast, check your stakes. They will be getting too close together. Spread them out. If the sides are leaning out too much, the stakes are getting too far apart too fast. Control the amount of space between the stakes, and you will control the shape.

1

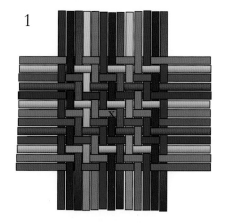

2

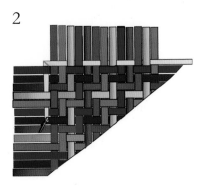

3

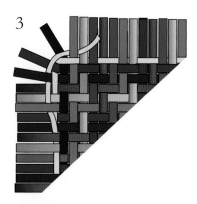

4

Photo of Pinching Corner

Photo Detail of Feet (or Ears)

The fullest point of this basket is about 8". The top diameter is 6". You must bring the diameter in two inches. There should be approximately 45 (optional number) rows of weaving.

To end the weaving, taper the weaver just as you began and end it just before the stake on which you started.

To avoid having an uneven rim, weave in a "false rim", i.e., weave one "start – stop" row of 3.8" flat reed, going over 2, under 2. See **DIAGRAM 5.** Overlap the ends 2 to 4 stakes. Push the row down or pull it up anywhere the top is not level.

INSERTING THE HANDLE:

Point all the outside stakes, bend them over to the inside and push them behind the first available row of weaving as in **DIAGRAM 6.** Cut all the inside stakes flush with the top row of weaving.

Insert the ears (with handle attached) into the weaving on the inside of the basket, with the center stakes directly across from each other, making the notch in the handle lie directly on the false rim. See **DIAGRAM 7.**

RIM:

Pre-measure the diameter of the inside of the basket and the outside. Add 3"- 4" to both measurements. Referring to **DIAGRAMS 8 & 9**, shave half the thickness from the bottom of the outer pieces and half from the top of the inner pieces. Place them on the basket with the overlaps near, but not on top of each other. Make sure both the overlaps are pointing in the direction you will be weaving. Place seagrass between the two rim pieces.

Hold everything in place with clothespins or clamps. With a long soaked piece of 11/64" flat oval reed hooked over the wall of the basket underneath the rim pieces, go into every or every other space from the outside to the inside. End the lasher as you began by hooking it over the basket wall and cutting it.

5

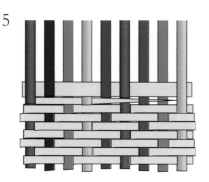

6

7

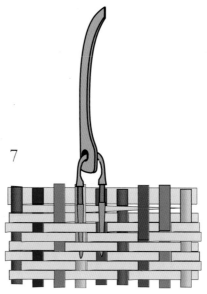

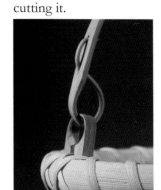

View of Hand Carved
Indian Swing Handle

8

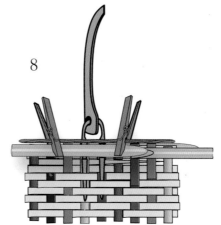

9

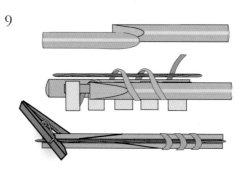

39

Derby Day Basket

by Anne Coleman

If you live in Kentucky, the first Saturday in May is a holiday. It is Derby Day, the running of the Kentucky Derby. To celebrate this event, Anne Coleman has designed a Derby Day Basket every year since 1997, and the Guild gathers on that Saturday to make the new design. This fun basket was from 2000. It is made over an easily obtainable mold and woven in a fast, continuous weave.

Approximate Size: 11" wide x 11" high x 8" deep
(May vary with the size of the mold)

MATERIALS and PREPARATION

1/2" flat reed (spokes for the back)
1/4" flat oval reed (spokes for ends and front)
3mm cane (lashing)
4mm cane (weavers)
11/64" flat reed (rim row)
1/2" flat oval reed (rim)
3.5' leather x 1/2" wide

5" x 10" oak base with groove
Horse Pin (see Facts about Contributors)

Cut 15 spokes 15" long from 1/2" flat reed for the back.
Cut 28 spokes 18" long from 1/4" flat oval reed for the sides.
Cut 26 spokes 20" long from 1/4" flat oval reed for the front.

To start this project, gather the regular basket-making tools
plus a hot glue gun and a mold for the basket.

The mold can be short like a plastic storage container for shoes, measuring about 6" x 11" on the bottom, or it can be a tall rectangular waste can about 7" x 11" on the bottom. See **DIAGRAM 1.**
Take a ruler with you and check out the local discount store.
The tall mold will be easier to use. When using the short mold, the bottom will have to be loosened and moved up as weaving progresses.

Hot glue the rectangular oak grooved base to the bottom of the mold with two dime size spots of hot glue. See **DIAGRAM 2.**

1

2

STARTING TO WEAVE:

Working with the mold "bottom side up", insert the spokes into the groove with their right sides up. The groove will be about 1/2" deep. Make sure the spokes are inserted all the way into the groove.

The 1/2" flat reed spokes will go into one of the long sides of the rectangular bottom. This will be the back of the basket. The 1/4" flat oval spokes will go into the short ends of the rectangle, 14 on each end. Crowd the spokes at the rounded corners and leave a little extra space in the center of each side. The rest of the 1/4" flat oval spokes (26) will go into the remaining long side which will be the front of the basket. See **DIAGRAM 3.**

3

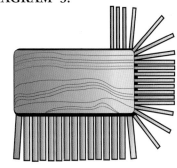

Begin weaving with 3mm cane, shiny side up. Taper the width of the end of the weaver to start (about half the width for a couple of inches) and insert it into the groove between spokes somewhere on the back. See **DIAGRAM 4.**

4

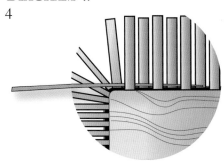

Because the mold is upside down, start the weaving in the opposite direction you would normally weave. When you turn the mold right side up, the weaving will be going in your usual direction. Notice that because

you have an odd number of spokes, you can do a continuous weave.

See "Basket Class" for more detail about continuous weave. Weave in plain weave, going over 1 spoke, under 1 spoke. Keep the row pushed up tightly against the wooden bottom. Check the spokes constantly, making sure they are pushed into the groove as tightly as possible. Keep enough tension on the cane weaver to keep the rows touching each other and the corners tight. Weave to the edge of the mold when the sides start to go up. Next sit and hold the mold in your lap with the wooden bottom facing your waist. Holding the mold this way puts pressure on the spokes and presses them against the mold as weaving continues. The weaving should be moving to the right now. Weave up to a height of 2" (measuring from the surface of the table as the basket sits).

Taper the end of a piece of 4mm cane to overlap with the 3mm. As the 3mm is ending, slide the new tapered end of the 4 mm on top of the old one and continue to weave with both for 4 spokes. Make sure the old end is not visible from the inside or the outside. See "Basket Class" for more detail of how to add a weaver. The weaving pattern changes now to a TWILL WEAVE, over 2, under 2. Weave to a height of 10 1/2" . See **DIAGRAM 5.**

5

As the weaving continues, keep the woven sides snugly against the mold. Make sure the corner spokes stay straight and the spokes in the center of each side do not bunch together. If you

are using a short mold, break the glue seal and move the mold up as needed. When 10" is reached, break the glue seal on the taller mold. A long awl can be inserted just above the wooden bottom to the inside through the weaving to pry up on the mold. First wet the area to be penetrated. See **DIAGRAM 6.**

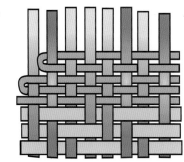

6

If you are using the short mold you will need to move it up in order to continue weaving. Do not remove the mold.

Switch back to 3mm cane and plain weave (over 1, under 1) for one row before beginning to weave the lapel. Weaving will no longer go all the way around the basket.

The ½" spokes will no longer be included. Weave to the last ¼" spoke. Then turn and weave back. The wrong side of the cane will be on the outside of the basket. Weave to the last ¼" spoke on the other side and turn and weave back, twisting the cane to keep the wrong side of the cane on the outside of the basket. See **DIAGRAM 7.**

7

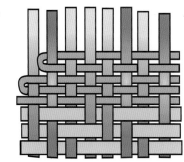

Turn on each ¼" end spoke one time. Each turn will happen on the spoke before the one that was turned on the previous row. Weave straight up, indenting one spoke each row.

In order to end up with a rounded lapel at the center (rather than a pointed one), do not turn on the last 5-10 rows. You must use your own judgment as to what looks best. Taper the end of the weaver to be nearly threadlike and let it run out behind a spoke.

Weave one row of 11/64" flat reed around the entire opening for the false rim in start-stop weaving. Start the weaver on the outside of a spoke, weave all the way around the basket and over the beginning of the weaver to the fourth spoke and cut it so it hides behind the spoke. See **DIAGRAM 8.**

8

Remove the mold. Dampen the ends of the spokes. ON THE BACK, bend the 1/2" spokes that are on the outside to the inside of the basket and tuck them behind several rows of weaving. Cut the remaining 1/2" spokes off flush with the top of the rim row.
See **DIAGRAM 9.**

9

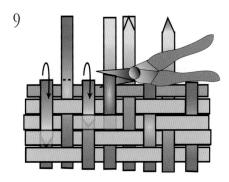

On the sides and the front, the 1/4" spokes that are on the inside of the weaving will fold and tuck to the outside of the basket and down into the weaving. Cut all the remaining 1/4" spokes even with the last row of weaving.

TURNING DOWN THE LAPEL:

The turn will take place where the 4mm twill weaving ends and the 3mm with the wrong side out begins. This area of the basket should be soaked in warm water for several minutes. When the spokes are soft enough to turn, bend the lapel over to the outside front of the basket. Do not fold. The curve of the reed to the outside should be gradual and well rounded. Do the turning in slow motion.

The turn will begin a few rows up from the twill weave. Shape slowly, getting the two sides of the turned area to match and the rounded center of the lapel to be in the center of the front of the basket.

Detail Photo of turned lapel

APPLYING THE RIM:

Use a ½" flat oval rim piece on the outside. This will cover the row of 11/64" reed. The flat oval will be on the outside of the basket on the back and on the under side of the lapel in the front. Shave the ends for about 2" so the overlapped area is no thicker than the regular single thickness of the reed. Place the overlapped area on the back of the basket. The piece of leather will go on the opposite side of the flat oval. It will be on the inside of the back of the basket and on the outside at the front lapel. Use #6 round reed between the rim pieces as a rim filler.
See **DIAGRAM 10.**

10

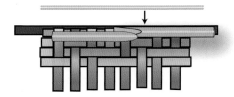

Lash the rims on with 3mm cane. Take the lasher into every space between spokes on the back (under the 11/64" rim row.) On the sides, take the lasher under the 11/64" and one row of cane to hide the folded reed. Lash in every space around the basket.
See Detail Photo of turned lapel.

FINISHING:

Decide where to place the wooden horse lapel pin. Do not attach the pin permanently until you are completely satisfied with the location.

Detail Photo of horse placement

Emily's Lit'l Pot Belly Purse

By Gail Hutchinson

This wonderful little purse was made by Gail Hutchinson of Milton, WV for her daughter, Emily, when she was a teenager. When it became too small for Emily, Gail took it back. Now she has designed a larger size for Emily and for the rest of us who need to carry a lot of "stuff". General directions are given for the smaller purse, but requirements are also listed for the larger one. Just substitute the different lengths.

MATERIALS and PREPARATION

SMALL VERSION of BASKET

3/8" flat reed	Cut: 9 pieces @ 16" long and 3 pieces @ 21" for stakes
11/64" flat oval reed	Cut: 2 pieces @ 17" for fillers
11/64" flat oval reed	Long piece for lashing
1/4" flat oval reed	20 pieces @ 20" for weavers
#2 round reed	1 very long piece for twining around the top
3/8" flat oval reed	For rim
Seagrass	
Leather for strap	

LID

3/8" flat reed	Cut: 7 pieces @ 8" and 3 pieces @ 10" for stakes
11/64" flat oval reed	4 @ 15" for fillers and 1 long piece for lashing
#2 round reed	1 @ approximately 80"
#4 round reed	1 @ 20"
3/8" flat oval reed	1 @ 21" for rim
Leather strip	1 @ 1/8" wide 8" long, 2 @ 1/4" wide 4" long with holes & 1 leather knot
Waxed linen	
Rivets (2 male and 2 female)	

LARGE VERSION of BASKET

5/8" flat reed	Cut: 3 pieces @ 26" and 9 pieces @ 21"
1/4" flat oval reed for fillers	2 pieces @ 20"
7mm flat oval reed for weavers	21 pieces @ 28" (the last four are tapered like the small purse)
#2 round reed	2 pieces @ 100"
1/2" flat oval reed	2 rims @ 29"
11/64" flat oval reed	Long piece for lashing
Seagrass filler	
Leather strap	

LID

5/8" flat reed	Cut: 3 pieces @ 20" and 7 @ 14"
1/4" flat oval reed	4 pieces @ 20" for fillers
#2 round reed	100+"
#5 round reed	Filler
3/8" flat oval reed	1 piece @ 29" for rim
11/64" flat oval reed	Long piece for lasher
Leather strip	1 @ 1/8" wide 8" long, 2 @ 1/4" long with holes & 1 leather knot
Waxed linen	
Rivets (2 male and 2 female)	

Dimensions: Small purse 6 1/2" wide x 5" high   Large purse 8 1/2" wide x 6" high

BASE:

Mark the centers of all the stakes on the wrong (rough) side. Soak your pieces before starting to weave. Lay out the nine 16" pieces of 3/8" marked side up, horizontally in front of you. Space the pieces to measure 6 ½". Using a 17" piece, weave under-over on the center marks. See **DIAGRAM 1.** With a piece of 11/64" flat oval reed (the filler), weave opposite the first piece, leaving a 5" tail on both ends. Bend the tails over and weave a second row overlapping where they meet. See **DIAGRAM 2.** Referring to **DIAGRAM 3**, repeat on the other side of the center piece (with the 11/64" flat oval). Now weave a 17" piece of 3/8" flat on both sides of the 11/64" flat oval. Now the base left to right consists of: 3/8", 11/64", 11/64", 3/8", 11/64", 11/64", 3/8". The base should measure: 6 ½" x 1 7/8".

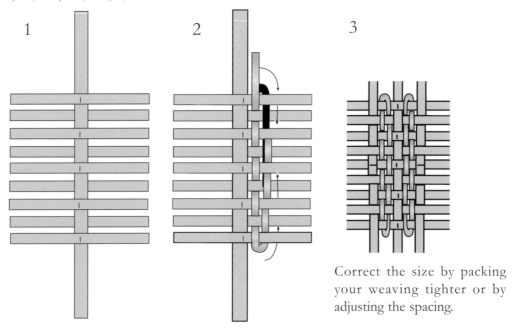

1   2   3

Correct the size by packing your weaving tighter or by adjusting the spacing.

SIDES:

Upsett only the back of this base and the back corners on each side. (There should be 11 upsett stakes).

See **DIAGRAM 4.**

Weave 10 start/stop rows, allowing the front stakes to flare while the back and back corners stand straight up. Pinch the back corner weavers and allow the front corner weavers to be rounded. Keep all the stakes evenly spaced applying pressure to the front and sides to make it go in ever so slightly. Make sure the back stays straight. Continue weaving 6 more rows.

The next four rows will "stair-step" toward the back of the purse as in **DIAGRAMS 5 AND 6.**

Taper the end of the ¼" damp flat oval reed lengthwise for about 4" to about half its normal width. See "Basket Class" for tapering info.

Looking at the front of the purse, start behind the #8 stake and weave over #9, round the corner, and U-O-U the side. Crimp the other back corner and weave U-O-U the side, round the front corner, over the #1 stake and behind #2. Stop. Unweave to the back corner and taper the weaver for about 4" just as you started. Reweave. Do the same thing for the next 3 rows, stepping back a stake for each row. Row 2 begins behind the 9th stake, row 3 behind the first side stake, row 4 behind the 2nd side stake.

Twine 2 rows with # 2 round by folding a long piece in half (actually a little off center). Each half becomes a "weaver". Take the top weaver behind the next stake. Then take the other weaver behind the next stake, etc. The twining will serve as the "false rim".

Point all the stakes, rewet them at the twining line and bend them to the inside, pushing them behind a couple of rows of weaving. See **DIAGRAM 7.**

RIMS:

Attach the leather strap on the center 3/8" stake on each side. Use a piece of waxed linen and secure the strap to the purse. Use either an awl to open up the space for the linen or thread a needle with the linen and sew it in place.

See **DIAGRAMS 8 AND 9.**

Place soaked 3/8" flat oval reed on the inside and outside, covering the #2 round reed twining. Make sure to overlap the ends at least 3". Shave the bottom of one of the overlaps for about 3" to half its thickness and the top of the other so the overlapped area is no thicker than a single thickness. **Make the top overlap point to the right** on both rim pieces. Lay a piece of seagrass between the two rim pieces as a filler. Overlap the ends of the seagrass about 1". Hold everything in place with clothespins. Place the overlaps NEAR but NOT ON TOP of each other.

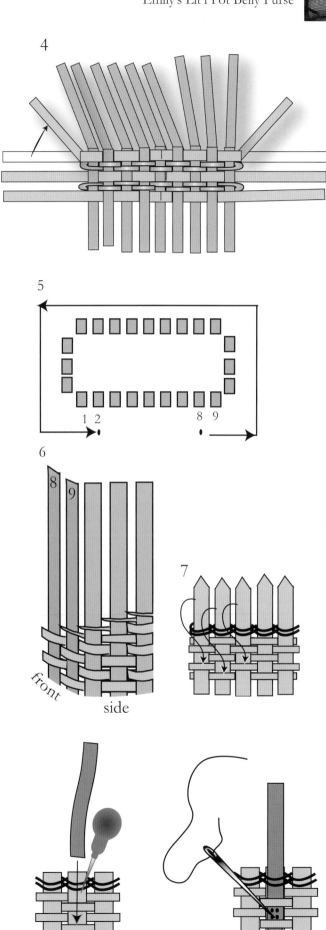

45

Begin the lasher by coming from the outside of the basket and "hooking" it over the basket wall as in **DIAGRAM 10**. Take the end into each space between stakes from the inside to the outside. When you finish lashing around the rim, turn and go back in the other direction, going into each space, to form an "X" lashing. End the lasher the same way it began, by "hooking" it over the wall under the rim pieces.

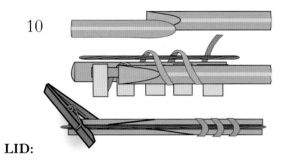

LID:

Make a template of the top of your purse. Place the purse "upside down" on a piece of paper and draw around it with pencil. Measure 3/8" inside of the mark all the way around. Cut the template out on the 3/8" mark. Lay seven 8" pieces of 3/8" flat reed, marked side up, horizontally in front of you. Use a 10" piece of 3/8" flat reed and weave it O-U aligning the center marks. Use a 10" piece of 11/64" flat oval reed and weave opposite the 3/8" row, leaving a tail on both ends. Fold the template in half strap to strap. This fold will be placed on the center spoke of the lid and give you a guide as to where to bend the 11/64" flat oval weaver. Bend the tails over to form a second row. Overlap the tails and cut off any excess. Repeat this process on the other side of the 3/8" piece. Keep referring to the template for size and to make sure your weaving stays within the size of the template. Every purse will be a little different measurement. Weave a 3/8" piece on both sides. Now, you must decide the front and back of the lid. The back will get another 11/64" flat oval with the same process. The front will also get the 11/64" filler, but only over the center 5 pieces of 3/8". When the weaving is finished, reading from the "FRONT" of your lid, the rows should be: 11/64", 11/64" (both over only 5 center stakes), (now over all 7 stakes) 3/8" 11/64", 11/64", 3/8" (center piece), 11/64", 11/64", 3/8", 11/64", 11/64". **See DIAGRAM 11.**

Lay the template again on the lid. Mark around it in pencil. This will be you first twine line. Twine one row around the lid. Twine around the 2 front corner stakes together as one, on both sides. This makes the front of the lid rounded instead of squared off. Do not cut weavers. Adjust the weaving to fill in the extra space. Your rows will be loose and not packed. Check to make sure the lid is about 1/4" smaller than the purse top all the way around. Twine a second row. Refer to the "Detail" photographs for clarification.

Point and tuck all the stakes to the bottom side (inside) of the lid. The only exception is the front corner stakes (the ones you twined together). Cut them off close to the twining. Be careful not to cut the twining.

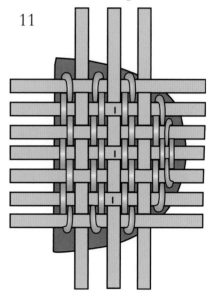

Clothespin the one piece of 3/8" flat oval to the #2 twining. Make sure you have about 3" of overlap. Make the rim stand upright (perpendicular to the weaving). Shave the overlapped area, top and bottom, so it is no thicker than a single thickness. Use #4 round reed for a filler that fits on the inside of the 3/8" rim piece (on top of the #2 round).

You will lash between the 2 rows of #2 twining, leaving a tail of 11/64" flat oval on the underside of the lid. Lash back in the other direction, making an "x" lashing. Tuck the beginning and ending tails into the underside of the lid.

"Detail"Photographs

The leather knot is tied on the center front of the purse just under the rim. The 8" leather strip is tied on the inside of the lid, around the center stake, next to the rim. See photos.

The 4" pieces of leather go around the lid and the purse rims in the back of the purse. Place the holes together and put the female and male rivets through the holes. With a hammer, hit the rivets to hold the leather together. All leather from Homestead Heirlooms 262-367-8739

Fabric Melon Basket

by Lyn Syler and Carolyn Kemp

Years ago, Deb Lorah of Pennsylvania gave Carolyn Kemp a lovely fabric woven melon basket. That little basket has inspired us to offer you an alternate weaving experience. Weaving with fabric makes this old style basket look different and new. Experiment with other fibers as well: perhaps yarn, ribbon, raffia or rope. The possibilities are endless. Enjoy the hassle free joy of weaving with fabric; it's easy on your hands and offers such a great decorating opportunity.

Dimension: 6" diameter

MATERIALS and PREPARATION

Two 6" round wooden hoops for rim and handle
#5 round reed for ribs
¼" flat reed for God's Eye and wrapped handle (wrapping is optional)
2-2 ½ yards of fabric for weavers
2' waxed thread for tying hoops
Basket stain, instant glue, fabric glue
Needle and thread (optional)

From the #5 round reed, cut six pieces 9" long for ribs. Shave or taper the ends for about ¾" with either a knife or a pencil sharpener (do not shorten the overall length of the ribs when you point them). See **DIAGRAM 1.**

Cut or tear strips of fabric 1 ½" wide, press and fold the edges together and then fold again as in **DIAGRAMS 2 & 3.** Using one length of folded fabric at a time makes it easy to weave. This avoids having to pull long pieces of fabric through the ribs. The strips can be easily joined as they run out.

1
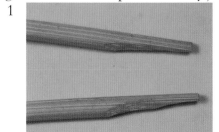

2
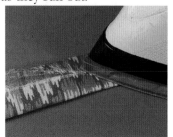

3

STAINING YOUR BASKET:

If you prefer a stained basket to a natural colored one, stain the weavers, hoops and ribs with your favorite basket stain. Select a natural wood color or one of the colors in your fabric. You must do the staining before starting to weave the basket.

After your materials are stained and dry, soak your ribs for about 15 minutes or until they are pliable.

Put your initials inside one of the hoops somewhere near the splice where the hoop is glued together. This hoop will be the basket handle and the initials will always be on inside of the bottom of the handle. Now take the second hoop and place it inside the first hoop. See **DIAGRAM 4**, this will be the rim of the basket. Make sure that the rim hoop is on the inside of the handle hoop. Using waxed string, tie the hoops together where they intersect, adjust if not centered. Cut off the ends of the waxed string.

WRAPPING THE HANDLE:
(optional)

If you want to wrap your handle with fabric, do so now.

WEAVING THE GOD'S EYE:

Select two long pieces of 1/4" flat reed. Coil them, secure with a bread tie and soak one now for 1-2 minutes. Follow the directions in **DIAGRAM 5** for starting the God's Eye. Be sure that the wrong (rougher) side of the reed is against the hoops as you weave the God's Eye. Refer to "Basket Class" for how to tell the right side of the reed from the wrong side. It does not matter on which side of the basket you start. It may be helpful to number the hoops

4

5

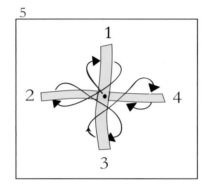

6

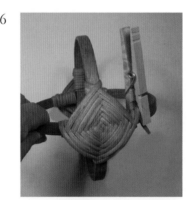

7

8

as in the diagram before you start. Think of the hoops as a clock face, number 1 is 12:00, number 2 is 9:00, number 3 is 6:00 and number 4 is 3:00. Begin the God's Eye by placing the wrong side of one weaver against the hoops where you have tied the waxed string. Hold the end of the weaver on top of the hoops, move up and behind 1, diagonally to 2 (now covering the end of the weaver), behind 2, diagonally to 3, etc. From 4 move diagonally to 1 and repeat entire counterclockwise revolution five more times. Pull the weavers tightly and press firmly as you make the revolutions, making sure the weaver is pressed completely flat against the hoops and the previous row. Use your thumbs to flatten the weaver as you work. You can check to make sure your revolutions are correct by counting the rows from the back of the God's Eye. The weaver should look like the photo of **DIAGRAM 6**, always going perpendicular on the back and diagonal on the front.

A good flat God's Eye is critical. Don't let the rows of weaving slip up on top of each other. The success of the basket depends on its construction. Don't be discouraged if your first try isn't perfect. Just take it out and try again.

At the end of the sixth revolution you will tuck the end of the weaver into the back of the God's Eye as pictured in **DIAGRAM 7**. On the back side, with the weaver dampened, cut the end to about ½", fold it at a 45 degree angle and push it under the weavers. You can add a dot of instant glue to secure it. Repeat the same process for weaving the other God's Eye.

INSERTING RIBS:

Taking one of the damp ribs, gently shape it by bending it with the natural curve of the round reed. The rib will slide in behind the God's Eye in the pocket formed between the rim and the lowest part of the handle on both sides. See **DIAGRAM 8**. If there seems to be too much pressure on the God's

Eye, remove the rib and round the shape a little more. You will place three ribs on each side of the lower halves of your rim. Space the ribs in equal thirds from the rim and the lower handle. Refer to **DIAGRAM 9** for the skeleton of the basket.

STARTING TO WEAVE:

Begin by inserting a folded strip of fabric under the weaver on the back side of the God's Eye, pushing it into the space between the weavers and the rim. Again, use a dot of instant glue to hold the fabric in place. Start the first row by coming up over the rim, under the first rib, over the number two rib, under the number three rib, over the lower handle and under and over the other three ribs and the rim. This row should be snug against the God's Eye, as in **DIAGRAM 10.** Continue weaving, snugging each row against the row ahead of it, covering the ribs as you weave. When your first strip of fabric starts to run out, fold the end back, so the cut edge is not showing. Take some fabric glue and hold the new strip and old strip together with a ½" overlap until the glue sets up. If you prefer to tack the pieces together with needle and thread, do so. Weave the new strip and then switch to the other side of the basket. Start the second God's Eye with a new folded strip of fabric and repeat the process you followed for the first eye. Weave until both sides of the basket are equal.

FILLING IN:

Weave additional fabric strips as needed, pushing or snugging the rows on the ribs to fill in the center section of the basket. Weaving with the fabric is fun and easy. There is so much "give" in the material that you are free of the rigidity of reed or other fibers. End your fabric strips by tucking the two strips into each other and either gluing them together or tacking them with needle and thread. See **DIAGRAM 11.**

9

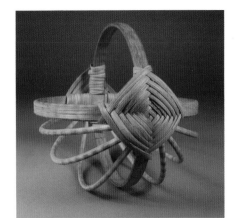

10

11

The Odyssey Gallery

The following eleven pages are filled with some of our favorite baskets made by weavers from all over the world. We owe special thanks to Joy Crook of Asheville NC and to Faye Clause of Maggie Valley NC for allowing us to photograph their personal basket collections, many of which are included here. We hope you enjoy this basket odyssey; a trip through the creative results of some wonderful basketmakers using a wide variety of materials and styles.

Carolyn Kemp "Antique Egg Basket" Original Watercolor

Arlene Moldrup Miniature Ash Backpack
1/2" x 1"

Lyn Syler "Odyssey I"
Ash with Pine Needle Rim

Two Lidded African Trinket Baskets from
Lagos, Nigeria
(Courtesy of Chandra Testman Ogunrinde)

Judith Olney "Cinquefoil"
Five-Way Quatrefoil

Judy K. Wilson Twined and Coiled Miniatures in Waxed Linen and Silk (right foreground)

Bob Coker Basket
with Bob Coker Handle and Rim
by Carolyn Kemp

Rowena Bradley
Miniature River Cane
Double Weave Basket
1" diameter x 3/4" high

Agnes Welsh Lidded Picnic Basket (lunch pail) Hand Split Dyed White Oak

Trevle Wood Key Basket
Hand Split White Oak

Oak Fish Baskets (Basketmaker Unknown)

Gertie Youngblood
Nested Oak Key Baskets

Judy Wobbleton
Hatteras Purse in Reed

Rowena Bradley Double Weave Lidded River Cane Series (4" largest, 2" smallest)

Carol Welch
Split White Oak Shoppers

Deanna Savoy
Lidded Nantucket Purse

JoAnn Kelly Catsos "Cherub"
Ash Basket with Lid

Jackie Abrams "Midare"
Hexagonal Weave with Random Interlacing
Cotton Paper, Paint, Varnish
Photography by Jeff Baird

Patti Quinn Hill "Anniversary 1"
Hand Painted Woven Archival Paper

Deanna Savoy "Christmas Round"

Deanna Savoy Pin Cushions

Master Basket Weavers - Kampala
Sosse Baker's African Trip 1993

55

Dee and Dennis Gregory Hand Split White Oak
Melon Baskets 12", 2" and 3/4" Diameter

Collection of Small River Cane and Honeysuckle Indian Baskets, Most Credited to Ramona Lossiah

Lyn Syler Miniature Collection 3" Melon Basket in
the Center with 1/2" melon in Front

Lyn Syler "Old Favorite" Market Basket
Space Dyed Reed

Marilyn Moore "Art Deco Vessel"
Twined Wire

Trevle Wood
Butterfly Basket
Hand Split White Oak Dyed

Judy K. Wilson Round Reed
"Buttocks" Basket

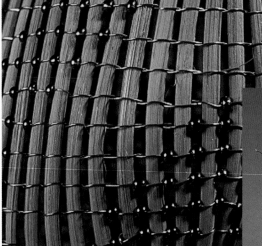

Linda Arter Sura "Tropical Wave"
Reed, Wire and Beads

Linda Arter Sura
Reed, Wire and Beads

Karen Bridgewater
Pine Needle Basket

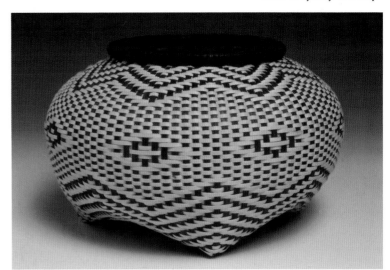

JoAnn Kelly Catsos "Diamonds & Snowflakes"
Ash

Patti Quinn Hill "Ancient Myths 1"
Hand Painted Woven Archival Paper

Bonnie Gale Willow Fishing Creel

Bonnie Gale Willow Backpack

Jimmie Kent
Ribbed Egg
Basket with
God's Eye

Nancy DeVries
"Basket Lady"
Mixed Media

59

Sosse Baker "Eyes of the Cattle"
Double Walled Flat Reed Basket
Photography by David Ryan

Nubian Basketmakers with Baskets
Sosse Baker in Africa 1993

Mary Lou Tierney "Trees"
Red Cedar Bark and Raffia

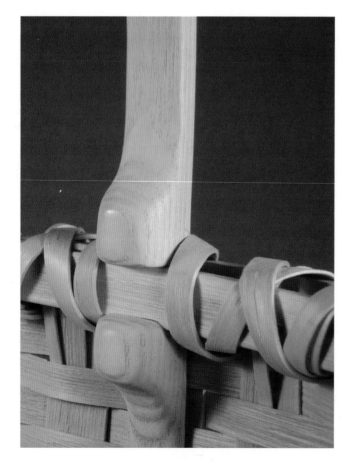

Jeffrey Gale Ash Market with Hand Carved Notched Handle

Lyn Syler Space Dyed Ash, Twill Weave
Market Baskets with Hand Carved
Poplin Hollow Indian Swing Handles

60

Flowing Twill Purse

By Wendy L. Reary

Wendy tells us that "Incorporating a twill such as this, just took using the right number of spokes to make the pattern repeat. I first saw this design on Judith Olney's basket 'Woven Weaving' ". Many thanks to Wendy Reary of Saint Louis, MO and to Judith Olney of Rowley, MA for this spectacular tote. It can be made in reed or any other workable material. You will be the main attraction carrying this!

Approximate Size: 10" x 2" base x 8" tall

MATERIALS and PREPARATION

2" x 9" rectangular wood base with groove
Spokes: ¼" flat reed - cut 48 spokes @ 10"
Weavers: 11/64" flat oval reed dyed black or dark brown
Rim row: ¼" flat reed
Rims: 3/8" half round reed
Rim filler: #6 round reed
Lashing: 4 ply waxed linen
Leather straps: ½" wide and whatever length you desire
2 beads to secure strap ends
Glue (optional)
Walnut stain

IMPORTANT: Before beginning, determine if you will be shimming or gluing the spokes into the base. The groove in the base will be the determining factor. If you find that your spokes slip and slide in the groove, you will need to secure them snugly before starting to weave. If the spokes are not VERY TIGHT, they will come out, and you will have a mess. Shimming is one option; gluing is the other. Because of the straight sides of the base, you will need to do one or the other. If you opt to glue, use a waterproof glue. Glue the spokes in place one day, let them dry overnight and re-wet them the next day by spraying when you are ready to weave the sides. If you use shims to hold the spokes in place, you can begin weaving right away. Your spokes will need to be damp to upsett them.

INSERTING SPOKES IN THE BASE:

With the wooden base on a flat surface, insert the spokes into the groove of the base; space them evenly, rough side up as follows: eighteen to each long side, one in each corner, and four on each short end. Secure them as described in Materials and Preparation.

See **DIAGRAM 1.**

1

You will upsett the dampened spokes as you weave. Each row is woven in the start-stop technique, i.e. each row begins on top of a spoke and ends by over weaving the beginning to the fourth spoke. See "Basket Class" for more information on start-stop rows.

STARTING TO WEAVE:

Note: it will take about four rows before you have caught all the spokes in the weaving pattern. With the start-stop rows, you may find that securing the rows with clothespins or small clips will be useful.

DIAGRAM 2 shows the first row of weaving, starting on the 2nd spoke in from the corner left front of the basket. Follow the graph (on the next page), starting with row one and reading the graph bottom to top.

ROW 1: Weave over 3, under 3, over 1, under 3, over 1, under 2, over 2, under 1, and repeat two more times.. (The pattern is 16 stakes and will be repeated three times around the basket for a total of 48 stakes on each single row).
Hide the end of the first weaver behind the second "under 3" as marked with an "X" in **DIAGRAM 2.**

Now, for row 2, start a new weaver on the back side of the basket, locating an OVER 3 (in row 1), and starting to weave directly above the OVER 3.

ROW 2: Reading from left to right, the second row of weaving will be: O2, U1, O2, U2, O1, U3, O1, U3, O1, repeated two more times around the basket. Check often to see that you have a repeat of 16 stakes. Remember that rows begin differently, some start with over, some with under; check the graph often to make sure you are on pattern.
Every fourth row will start the same place on the basket as did row 1. It is extremely helpful to write the pattern count every row. The pattern consists of 16 stakes times three for a total of 48 stakes, and 16 rows of weaving up the sides.
Row 17 will start the pattern over again. Weave a total of 40 rows (2 ½ pattern repeats.). The shape is up to you. Generally, the sides should be rather straight from bottom to top.

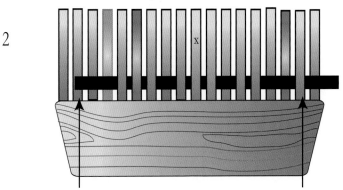

2

Pattern for 1-16 stakes on the first row, repeated three times for a total of 48 stakes

PATTERN GRAPH

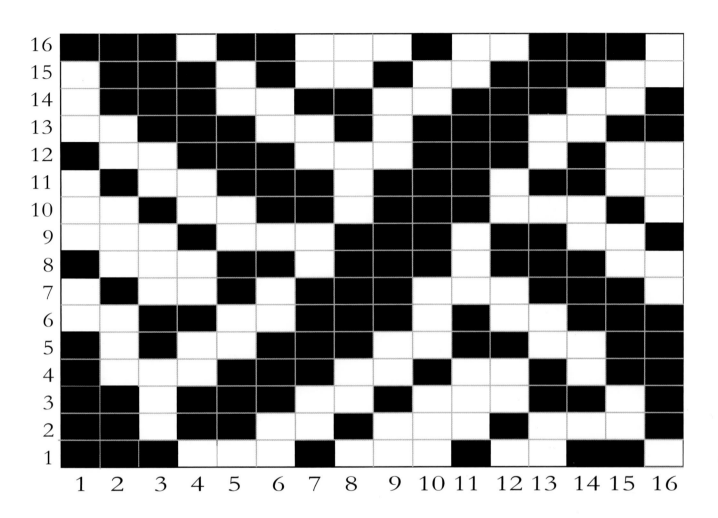

■ over   □ under

FALSE RIM ROW:

3

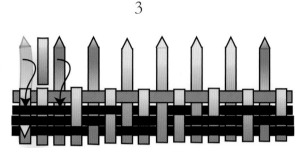

The top row should be a false rim row of ¼" flat reed, woven over one, under one.

Pack all the rows of weaving down very tightly. Looking at the basket from the inside, point all of the stakes that are on the outside of the rim row and tuck them to the inside behind one or two rows of weaving. Cut all the stakes that are on the inside flush with the top of the rim row. See **DIAGRAM 3** (view from the inside of basket).

RIM:

Measure the circumference of the top of the basket and add about 4" for overlap. Cut a piece of 3/8" half round reed that same length. This is for the outside rim piece. The inside rim piece will be approximately 1" shorter. Soak the rims until they are very flexible. Clip the rims in place on the basket. Mark the area of overlap. Remove the rims and shave half the thickness from the top of one and the bottom of the other so they will fit together smoothly as in **DIAGRAM 4.**

Both the rim overlaps should be pointed to the right (if you lash to the right, to the left if you lash to the left).

When you replace the rim pieces, the overlaps should be placed near, but not on top of each other. See **DIAGRAM 4A.** Use two small pieces of leather or several thicknesses of ½" flat reed as spacers on the short ends (centered) to provide a space for the leather strap. Place the spacers between the rims where the strap will go. See **DIAGRAM 5.**

4   4A   5

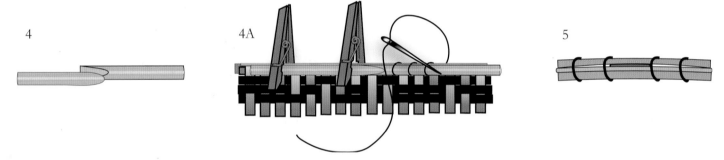

Fill the space between the rims with #6 round reed, beveling the ends for a smooth overlap. Lash the rim in place with the waxed linen threaded on a large tapestry needle or by itself. Make a space with an awl between the stakes before threading the waxed linen. Hook the lasher over the basket wall, under the rim pieces, or just tie it on. Go into every space between stakes the to the right. At the end of the rim, turn and repeat in the other direction, creating an X pattern with the lasher.

STAINING THE BASKET and FASTENING THE LEATHER STRAP:

Stain your basket using your favorite walnut stain; the dyed reed will not be affected to any degree, but the natural undyed stakes will take on the walnut color.

Poke a small hole at each end of the leather strap, ½" from the end. Remove the spacers. Insert the strap end between the rim and the outside of the basket. The end of the strap should extend down about 1" below the top. Thread a bead with waxed linen. Put both ends of the thread through the hole in the strap, through the wall of the basket and on either side of one of the center end stakes. See **DIAGRAM 6**. Tie the ends together securely on the inside of the basket. Repeat on the other side.

6

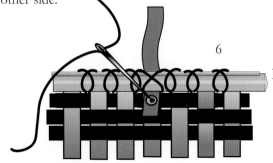

You have now finished your
Flowing Twill Purse, and you are
VERY HAPPY !

Natural Vine Wall Basket

by Faye Clause

This great natural basket is ours compliments of Faye Clause of North Carolina and Florida. Faye would encourage you to use hers only as a guide and to experiment with other natural materials as well. You will be amazed at your own creativity!

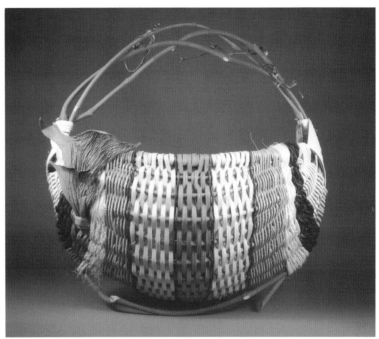

Dimension: approximately 13" diameter

MATERIALS and PREPARATION

Grapevine for making handle hoop, approximately 10' - 12'
#6 round reed for rim and ribs

Suggested materials for weaving:
11/64" flat reed for weavers, some dyed and some natural
Philodendron sheaths
Dyed # 3 or #4 round reed for weavers
Palm inflorescence, honeysuckle, Virginia creeper, jute twine or
    leather for additional weavers, or any natural material of your choice

Preliminary Step:
Soak the Philodendron sheaths at least six hours or until they are pliable, then wrap them in a towel until you need them.
From the grapevine, construct a circular frame that is approximately 13" in diameter.
Twist the vine around itself and secure the ends by tucking them into each other. See **DIAGRAM 1.**
Next, soak a long piece of #6 round reed that is long enough to form the "D" part of the frame twice (approximately 65").
Bend the reed to fit about 2" above the center of your round frame. Form the "D" with the opening about 4.5" in the center. Twist the reed around another time to make it stronger. See **DIAGRAM 2.**
Place the "D" frame rim inside the grapevine frame and secure with twist ties or waxed linen. See **DIAGRAM 3.**

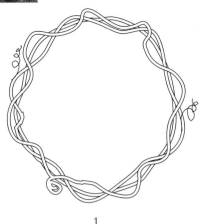

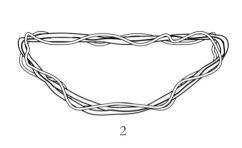

1

2

3

MAKING THE GOD'S EYE:

Soak a long piece of 11/64" flat reed (or #3 round reed), the color of your choice, until it is pliable. As in **DIAGRAM 4,** begin with the weaver on top of the frame at the dot. Move it up and behind 1, diagonally to 2, behind 2, diagonally to 3, behind 3, diagonally to 4, and behind 4. From 4, move to 1 and repeat the entire counter clockwise procedure 6 more times

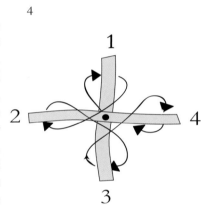

4

or until the God's Eye is large enough to hold the points of the ribs. See **DIAGRAM 5** for a finished God's Eye.

Do not cut the weaver that remains, but secure it at the rim with a clothespin. You will need this to begin your weaving around the ribs. Repeat the process on the other side with another long soaked weaver.

The ribs in this basket must be measured by "sighting" them because of the irregular shapes of the grapevines. Every one's will be a little different. It isn't difficult to "eyeball" the shape that you want your basket to have. Look at **DIAGRAM 6** for basic shape. Remember that you want the back of the basket to be very FLAT, but you want the front to have the shape of a "nest" or a "pouch." The ribs must gradually become longer as they are farther down the front of the basket. See **DIAGRAM 7.**

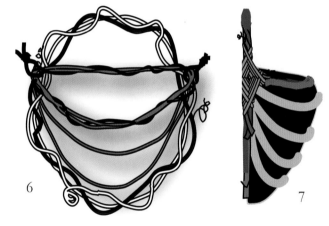

6

7

5

NOTICE on the inside of the God's Eye, there is a pocket, a place for you to position the ends of the ribs. Point the ends of the ribs either with a knife or scissors on a slant for about an inch. The tapered sides of the ends of the ribs will lie next to each other, helping to hold the ribs in place. See **DIAGRAM A.**

A

First, put four ribs in place, two in front of the basket and two in back. Generally, the #1 front rib should protrude from the rim about 1". Next, place the bottom front rib in front 1.5" from the bottom of the grapevine. Place the #1 back rib approximately 1" from the top of the rim. Place the #2 back rib about 1" from the grapevine bottom. Don't forget to keep the back FLAT.

WEAVING:

Now you are ready to start weaving. Dampen the reed that remains from making the God's Eye and begin weaving over and under the rim, the two front ribs, the bottom of the grapevine, the two back ribs, and the back rim. Turn around on the rim and weave back in the opposite direction. Weave a few rows on each side, then insert two more ribs in the front of the basket. One goes under the top (initial) rib and the other goes above the bottom one. Also add two new ribs on the back, one under the top rib and one above the bottom. KEEP BACK RIBS FLAT. Continue to weave with the same weaver the God's Eye was made from for about 2" more. Add more ribs as you need them. Hint: Anytime two of your finger's width will fit between ribs, you need to add another one.

Now repeat the same weaving from the God's Eye on the other side of the basket.

When you have woven approximately 4" on the bottom grapevine rim, put a new rib in to take its place. Do not use the grapevine rim at the bottom of the basket as a rib any more. See **DIAGRAM 8.** Put the rib in between the bottom front and the bottom back ribs. This is optional and you may want to keep weaving around the grapevine for a different look.

Change color and size of reed and materials as often as you would like.

To add in a new material or a new piece of any kind, lay the new piece in with the old and weave with both for <u>four</u> ribs. Then continue with only the new one. Just make sure the old one ends up on the inside of the basket, under a rib. Be sure to put enough ribs in to have a nice and sturdy shape. Remember to alternate sides of the basket, changing weaving material to suit your taste.

Take one soaked Philodendron sheath, split it in half and place one half on the left side of the opening between the rim and the first rib.

Place the other (half) sheath to the right of the first one, starting it one rib down from the other.
See **DIAGRAM 9.**

Now, twine both ends of the sheaths together all the way down the front and around to the back. It may take part of another sheath added on to reach around to the back.
Finish your basket by weaving the center, unwoven space with whatever material you wish. Use honeysuckle or Virginia creeper or round reed to add a new texture and coloration to the weaving. You cannot do anything "wrong"; the choices are up to you and result in a different look to every basket. Just have fun!

9

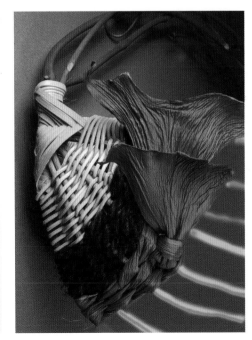

8

Detail of Center Section

67

On the Contrary

By Lyn Syler

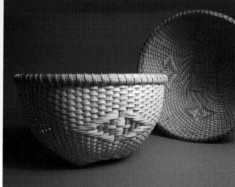

Dimensions: Approximately 8" Diameter x 7" High

On the Contrary is a replication of an old imported basket that my friend Faye Clause had for many years. It waited patiently for years for me to copy it; it is pictured here in the background of the photograph above and right. I have made it in several variations; natural stakes and weavers, dark stakes and light weavers. It is always nice. The important thing about this basket is that it is woven with a continuous weave. It needed extremely narrow stakes, so I made it in oak and ash. It can also be made in reed with the same directions, just longer stakes. The title refers to my return to weaving after a long absence and how quickly a negative can become a positive.

MATERIALS and PREPARATION

1/8" Ash or Oak for stakes
1/8" Ash for weavers
3/8" Oak or Ash for false rim
Oak or Ash 1/2" flat oval for rims or dyed pine needles for alternate rim treatment
Waxed linen or 1/8" Ash for lashing
Sweetgrass or pine needles for rim filler

The ash and oak are very fragile and require being damp at all times. Not WET, but dampened with a slight spray or sponge. Treat them gently to avoid breakage. From 1/8" stake material, cut 34 pieces 16" long and one piece 8" long.

THE BASE:

Lay 17 of the 16" pieces horizontally in front of you and weave the other 17 pieces in vertically in a 3/3 twill. See **DIAGRAM 1.**

1

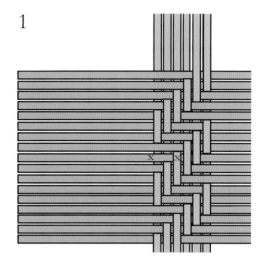

If there is a right and wrong side, (usually there is not) lay the right side up. The first piece, with the center marked, goes on top of the center of the horizontal piece. Line up center marks. Reading from the bottom up, the weaving pattern for the first vertical row is: O1, U3, O3, U3, O3, U3, O1
Row 2: O2, U3, O3, U3, O3, U3
Row 3: O3, U3, O3, U3, O3, U2
Row 4: U1, O3, U3, O3, U3, O3, U1
Row 5: U2, O3, U3, O3 ,U3, O3
Row 6: U3, O3, U3, O3, U3, O2

After these 6 rows are in place, repeat the pattern beginning with Row 1 to the right. The weaving to the left of the center is in reverse order, i.e., the next row to the left is a repeat of row 6, the next row 5, next row 4, etc. Follow this pattern until all 17 pieces are in place.The base is done and lying RIGHT side up.

2

STARTING TO WEAVE:

Taper the full length of one 1/8" weaver (enough to go around the base two times). The tapered weaver should be about one half its original width. Begin the tapered weaver just after a corner and weave opposite the base; weaving all the way around one time, mitering the corners (a 45 degree angle fold). Weaving opposite the base weaving locks everything in place. Refer to "Basket Class" for mitering instructions. See **DIAGRAM 2.** Do not cut the weaver, but continue weaving, changing at the starting point to an over 2, under 2 pattern. Ignore the locking row. Nothing matches the locking row.

3

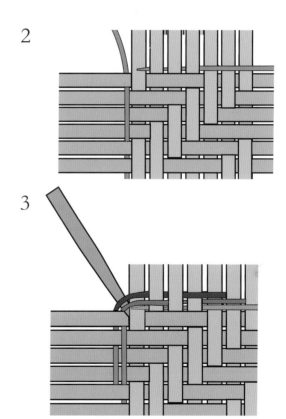

When you have reached the starting point again, insert the short stake (to create an odd number of stakes and enable you to do a continuous weave) in the corner, hiding the end under the base weaving. This extra stake will "throw off" the weaving pattern so the over 2's will step over one stake each row. See **DIAGRAM 3.**

Continue to weave with the base lying flat on a table surface, over 2, under 2 for six rows. As you weave rounds, pinch the corners and spread ("starburst") the stakes from the center of the side to the left and right, filling in the corners with stakes. All the corners must be filled with stakes that are equidistant from each other. As you spread the stakes, the base will naturally start to get peaks or the cat-head shape at the corners. You may encourage that process by pulling tighter than usual on the weaver as you round the corners. See **DIAGRAM 4.**

4

ADDING A NEW WEAVER WHEN ONE RUNS OUT: Add weavers as needed by hiding the end of a new wet weaver behind a stake and weaving with the two until the old one runs out. Cut the end of the old piece so it doesn't show from the inside. See "Basket Class" for details on adding a new weaver.

AT THIS POINT:
MARK SIDE 1: The side with the added stake in the left corner
MARK SIDE 2: Rotate the basket 90 degrees
MARK SIDE 3: Opposite side 1
MARK SIDE 4: Opposite side 2

On side one, just after the added stake, change to over 1, under 1 (plain weave).

NOTE: The first row of plain weave will be easy. The second row will be more difficult. Spread the stakes to allow more room as needed. If the weaving is impossibly tight, leave the base flat on the table for another row or two. After the second or third row of plain weave, lift the base off the surface. Just the fact that it is lifted off the table will make the sides automatically start to go upright.

Watch the shape that is emerging. Make sure all the sides are leaning evenly. Adjust the stakes and pack rows down tightly as you go. The secret of shaping success is to keep the stakes evenly spaced. If you feel the spaces are getting wider, check to see if the sides are leaning outward more. Likewise, if the spaces are getting tighter, the sides are probably going in.

Weave four rows of plain weave.

THE PATTERN:

Locate and mark the center stake on all four sides. Remember, one side will have an extra stake so when finding the center of that side the count will be "off" one stake.
Referring to the Pattern Graph: The 14th row will be the first pattern row although nothing different happens. Just be sure that the weaver goes under the center stake on sides one and three and over the center stake on sides two and four.
Row 15 is also plain weave.
Row 16 begins the pattern **changes.** Looking at the graph, weave the next 12 rows. Remember that like a quatrefoil, the same things happen on sides one and three and two and four **within the same row.** Watch to see when a new row begins with side one. It's hard to do, because you tend to become absorbed in the pattern, but don't forget to check on your shaping.

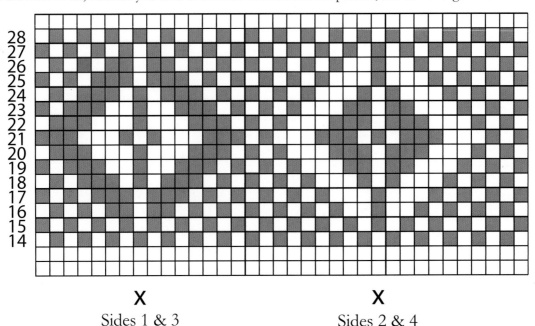

X
Sides 1 & 3

X
Sides 2 & 4

NOTE: The pattern will be positive on two sides and negative on the other two. i.e. the "overs" in the first diamond will be "unders" on the other two sides.

Remember that everything is plain weave except the center diamond. Whatever you do to side one, you will do also to side three. Likewise with sides two and four.

After all the pattern rows are done, weave four or five rows (or as many as you want) of plain weave and taper the end of the weaver so it runs out above the starting point on side one. Weave one row of rim filler (3/8") going over and under two or three stakes at a time.

Dampen the ends of the stakes and bend all the outside stakes to the inside. Cut them so they are hidden behind the rim filler or push them behind one of the rows of weaving. Bend the inside stakes over to the outside and either push them behind a row of weaving or cut them flush with the bottom of the false rim row. See **DIAGRAM 5.**

APPLYING THE RIM:

You probably have noticed that our basket has been photographed with two different rim treatments; the more traditional wooden rim and the lashed pine needle rim. You can decide which one you like best. Detailed instructions for each are given in the "Basket Class" section.

5

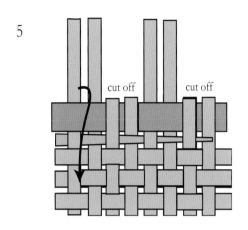

The photograph above shows the pattern repeated three times up the sides (vertically) as well as around the basket. If you want to make this version, then start with longer stakes and repeat the pattern as many times as you want.

Pathways in Reed

by Lyn Syler

For some time I had been thinking about all the possible paths there are for each of us and about what makes us choose a certain path. As usual, for me, a basket is the eventual expression of my thoughts and convictions. Make this lovely basket in one or all of the options given. If you want five "paths" instead of three, the numbers are given below. If you want the shorter "fruit bowl" style, just shorten the spokes a little. Let your creative energy run wild and ENJOY !

Note: This basket can be made with five spirals instead of three. Cut 27 pieces, cut them each in half, now you have 54. Weave the pattern as follows: O/U for ten times, then O2, U/O for nine times and O2 for the rest of the basket. There will be no need to weave the O2 at the end of the first row since there is an even number of spokes. Simply keep on weaving around again for another row. To reverse the spiral simply move the "Over 2" back two spokes at the O2 where the weaving started and repeat at every O2 thereafter, making the two's spiral in the other direction.

Pattern Basket Made by Suzanne Moore

Dimensions: 10 1/2" diameter x 6 1/2" high (plus handle)

MATERIALS and PREPARATION

1/2" flat reed (spokes)
11/64" flat oval reed (weavers and lashing)
3/8" flat reed (rim row)
1/2" half round or flat oval (rim)
Seagrass (rim filler)
5" wooden base with slot for spokes
10" stationary handle or side grip handles or swing handle (directions for all variations)
CUT: From 1/2" flat reed, 26 pieces 12"-14" long

Handle and base available from Suzanne Moore, NC Basket Works, POB 744, Vass NC 28394
1-800 338-4972 www.ncbasketworks.com

BASE:

The entire basket will be woven from the outside, so the BOTTOM (flat side) of the base should be UP when you begin inserting the spokes. Insert the spokes RIGHT SIDE UP.

Insert all the spokes into the groove around the edge of the base, adjusting the width of the spokes when necessary so they all fit in comfortably with about 1/8" between them. See **DIAGRAM 1. Soak** a long piece of 11/64" flat oval reed until it is pliable. Taper the end for about 3" so it is almost threadlike at the beginning. Start the "skinny" end of the weaver, RIGHT SIDE UP, anywhere and weave over 1, and under 1, all 26 spokes. Leave the base lying on a table with the OUTSIDE of the base up. Make a mark on the end of the starting spoke so it will be easier to locate when ending the weaving. See **DIAGRAM 2**. After you have made one complete row of weaving, and are back at the starting spoke, weave over 2 spokes and then go back to weaving over 1, under 1.
See **DIAGRAM 3**.

Stop at this point and cut all the spokes in half lengthwise. Resume weaving using all 52 spokes.
The last **stroke** (see GLOSSARY) at the starting point was under, so the first stroke with the split spokes is over.. Weave over 1 and under 1 (plain weave) for 16 spokes.
See **DIAGRAM 3A.** Weave OVER spokes 17 and 18. Then continue plain weave for 15 spokes, and again weave over 2. Continue plain weave again for 15 spokes and again weave over 2. Use this pattern for the rest of the basket.
The over 2's will automatically advance one spoke and the plain weave will be opposite the previous row. You must spread the spokes apart as quickly as possible so there is enough room between them for the weaver to fit in comfortably.
Leave the base lying flat for 6-8 rows of weaving. Then lift it off the table and without applying any pressure to the spokes, continue weaving. The spokes will begin to "round" upward without your help just because they are no longer lying on a flat surface. Check the shape you are getting frequently. Apply more tension to the weaver if you want the sides to go straighter up. Relax the tension if you want them to flare more.
Mindless weaving won't produce a particular shape or top diameter. You must be in control !

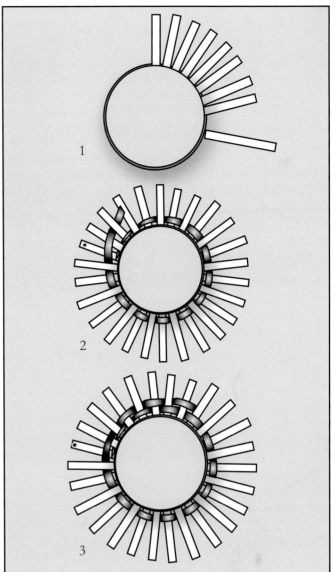

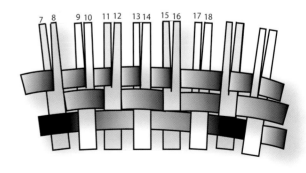

3A

HELPFUL HINT:

On any basket, there is a certain relationship between the shape of the basket and the amount of space between the spokes. As a general rule, if you want the sides to lean out, you need more space between spokes. If you want the sides to go straight up or to lean inward, there must be less space between the spokes. If you are weaving happily along on this basket and you realize one side is leaning out or in too much, check the space between the spokes. Constantly adjust the position of the spokes to be sure they are equidistant for a smooth, even shape.

When a weaver runs out, add another weaver by ending the old one on top of a spoke. Place the end of a new soaked weaver on top of the old one, overlapping the two ends for four spokes. Make sure the end of the new one is hidden behind a spoke as in **DIAGRAM 4.**

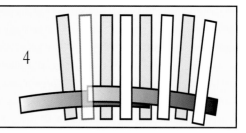

4

You will keep weaving the sides of the basket until the desired height is reached. The basket in our photograph has 47 rows of weaving.

End the weaving directly above the starting point, behind the same spoke where it started. Taper the end for several inches before ending and make it end in an almost thread-like width at the end. See **DIAGRAM 5.**

Weave one start-stop row of 3/8" flat reed weaving in plain weave (or if that is too tight, weave over and under 2 spokes at a time.) Overlap the weaver on the last four spokes and cut off at the end so the weaver is hidden behind the 4th spoke.

Dampen the ends of the spokes and cut the inside spokes flush with the top of the false weaver and bend the outside spokes (tapered to a point) to the inside, tucking the end behind the first available weaver. See **DIAGRAM 6.**

Insert the stationary handle on the spokes that are directly across from each other. If you are using two side handles or ears with a swing handle attached, insert them on either side of the center spoke on both sides. See **DIAGRAMS 7 and 7A.**

Soak a long piece of ½" half round (or flat oval) reed. Measure the circumference of the top of the basket. Add 2½"-3" for the outside rim. Cut another piece that is 2½" shorter for the inside rim. Shave the ends of the overlapped area so it is no thicker than a single piece of the half round reed. (Shave the top of one end and the bottom of the other at the area to be overlapped.)

Use **DIAGRAM 8** as reference for the following steps.

Place the rim pieces on the basket, making sure the overlapped ends are pointing in the same direction. Place the overlaps NEAR, but not on top of, each other. Add a piece of seagrass between the two rim pieces. Hold the rim pieces in place with cable ties or clothespins. With a long soaked piece of 11/64" flat oval reed, begin lashing, starting just past both the overlaps. "Lose" the lasher by pushing one end up under the inside rim, over the basket wall, and down under the outside rim. Lash the rim in place by taking the other end into the spaces between spokes (under and around the rim). End the lasher, losing it inside the rim as it began.

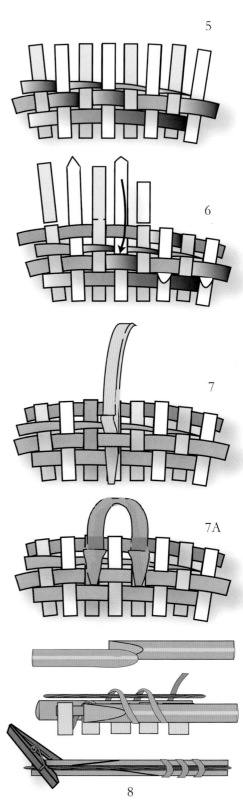

5

6

7

7A

8

Plaid of Many Colors

by Lyn Syler

The wonder of pattern is showcased here. A basket in the Qualla Arts and Crafts Co-op in Cherokee, North Carolina was my inspiration for this basket many years ago. Interestingly, the pattern is the same theory as a Shaker quatrefoil, just made in a different configuration. Not much is really "new" in basketmaking. Enjoy making your own "Plaid of Many Colors," perhaps with your own colorways. It is also elegant in all natural. Try it with dark natural stakes and light natural weavers.

Dimensons: 7" x 7-1/2" Base x 9" High

MATERIALS and PREPARATION

7mm flat oval reed or 1/4" flat reed - use heavier reed for stakes/lighter for weavers
5/8" flat oval reed - for rim
11/64" flat or flat oval reed - for lasher
Seagrass - rim filler

Dye the 7mm or 1/4" reed for stakes and weavers
    green
    red
    blue
    gold (weavers only, no gold stakes)

Cut 16 pieces each of red, blue, green - each 32" long (for stakes)

LAYING OUT THE BASE:

Dampen all the stakes and mark centers on the wrong side.
Lay 23 pieces horizontally in the order shown in
DIAGRAM 1.

> Center five are RED
> Above and below center red four BLUE
> Above and below blue four GREEN
> Above and below green one RED

Referring to **DIAGRAM 1A**, weave five reds vertically in a 3/3 twill, aligning center marks. The center vertical red stake should line up with the center horizontal red stake. Following the established twill, weave 4 rows of blue to the right of the 5 red stakes. Note: Diagram 1A only pictures one blue stake.

Using **DIAGRAM 2** as a guide, weave four blue pieces to the left of the center five red pieces. Note: Once six pieces are woven, all you have to do is count back six pieces and repeat the 3/3 twill pattern. Repeat the same procedure with the remaining green stakes, weaving four green stakes to either side of the four blue stakes. Last, weave two red pieces on the right and on the left. The finished base is shown in **DIAGRAM 2.**
It should measure 7" x 7-1/2"

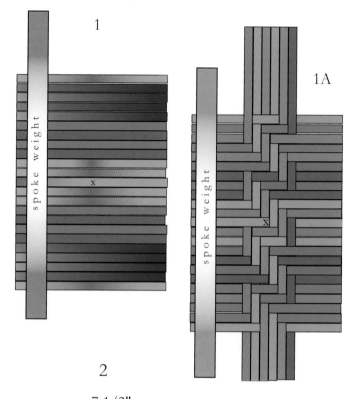

1

1A

spoke weight

spoke weight

2

7 1/2"

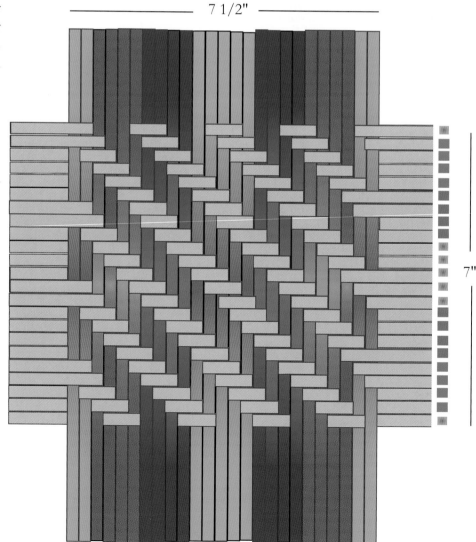

7"

UPSETT THE BASE:

Dampen the stakes and gently "upsett" your basket. See "Basket Class" for complete description of how-to upsett.

WEAVING THE SIDES:

The sides are woven in the following colors: (Reading the graph, PICTURED BELOW, bottom to top)
    4 rows blue, 4 rows green, 4 rows red, 5 rows gold, 4 rows red, 4 rows green, 2 rows blue

The sides are woven in start/stop rows; start every row on a different side of the basket to avoid heavy build up in one area. Begin the first row of weaving by locating the center red stake on any side as in **DIAGRAM 3.**

ROW 1: O1 (the center red stake on any side) *U2,O2,U2,O2,U2, O3 (3 corner red stakes) U2,O2,U2,O2,U2,O1(the center of three red stakes) and repeat from * until you reach your starting point. End the row by overlapping four pairs of stakes, hiding the weaver behind a stake. See "Basket Class" for start/stop.

Note: The centers of all sides and the corners are all over 1, over 3, under 1, or under 3. Only the order in which they occur is different.

You will be weaving this basket so that the sides are relatively straight up.

ROWS 2 - 27: FOLLOW THE GRAPH FOR THE WEAVING PATTERN

There are 27 start/stop rows of weaving in this basket.

Graph rows 1 - 27

FINAL TWO ROWS:

After all 27 rows are woven according to the graph, weave the last two rows (28 & 29) in blue by weaving over 3, under 3 as in **DIAGRAM 4**. Push the stakes together and treat the three as one. These last two rows will be covered by the rim. Cut the stakes on the inside of the last row of weaving. Cut two of the three on the outside. Point one and push it to the inside, hiding the end behind a weaver as in **DIAGRAM 5**

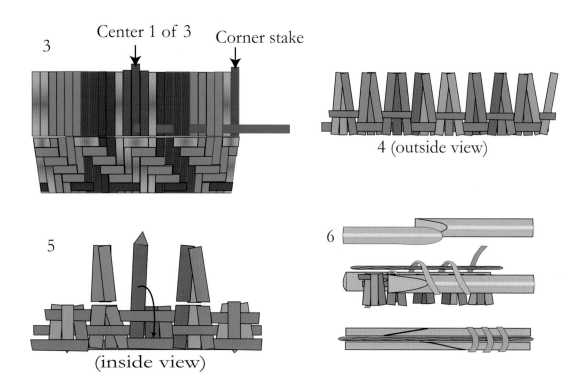

3   Center 1 of 3   Corner stake

4 (outside view)

5   (inside view)

6

RIM:

Rim with 5/8" flat oval, lashing between all the sets of stakes or every other set.
See **DIAGRAM 6**. See "Basket Class" for a more detailed description on rimming.

Note: The photograph at the right is a detail of the basket woven in all natural color ash. The pattern is very subtle but elegant.

Points of Light

by Lyn Syler

Dimensions: 4" x 4" Base x 9" High

I walk a labyrinth every day that I can. It is the most ancient of meditation tools. One day as I walked, I kept seeing spots of light that actually were the sharp turns of the labyrinth path. The image remained with me so I made Points of Light remembering that years ago I had seen a basket by Sosse Baker that left "spots" unwoven. So now every time I look at Points of Light, I think of my labyrinth. The Energy of Creativity often appears when I least expect it. The experience of writing the directions was challenging since every "point" is a little different….but since when have "we" been daunted by a little challenge?

MATERIALS and PREPARATION

7mm flat oval reed (or ¼" heavy ash) stakes
11/64" flat oval reed (or 1/8" heavy ash) weavers
3/8" flat reed (or 3/8" heavy ash or oak) false rim
Dyed or natural pine needles for rim (or rim material of your choice)
Waxed linen for lashing rim and large tapestry needle
11/64" flat oval reed (or 1/8" ash or oak or waxed linen) lashing
Dye the stake material black or the color of your choice
Dye pine needles if desired

WEAVING THE BASE:

From the stake material, cut 26 pieces approximately 26" long. The base is woven in a 2/2 twill. (In the case of very heavy reed, you may want to use a 3/3 twill base). Lay 13 pieces horizontally with centers marked on the right side.

Weave the first piece, from the bottom up, o2, u2, o2, u2, o2, u2, o1.

Row 2: u1, o2, u2, o2, u2, o2, u2

Row 3: u2, o2, u2, o2, u2, o2, u1

Row 4: o1, u2, o2, u2, o2, u2, o2

These four rows are repeated to the right (for 3 rows) and to the left in reverse (for 6 rows).

The base should resemble **DIAGRAM 1.**

Measure and "true" the base to approximately 4" x 4".

FORMING THE CAT-HEAD BASE:

Taper one end of a long soaked weaver to half its width, with the taper long enough to reach around the base.

Then, as in **DIAGRAM 2**, with the base flat on a table, right side up; weave around the base, over 2, under 2, (a locking row) for one row only. See "Basket Class" for detailed instructions on weaving a locking row.

On the second row, begin the pattern stroke, over 2, under 1, and begin to "pinch" the corners. By the 5th row the corner spaces will be filled in with stakes. See **DIAGRAM 3.**

Pinch the corner stakes together and lift up on the corners as you weave around.

As you are holding the corners up and together, pull firmly on the weaver to keep the stakes in place.

If the "feet" (or "ears") aren't pronounced enough for you, place your thumbs in the corners (from the inside) and push the corners out. Wet and weight any side that isn't cooperating to make it sit straight.

Resume weaving until there are 8 or 9 rows.

Add weavers as needed by hiding the end of a new wet weaver behind a stake and weaving with the two until the old one runs out. Cut the end of the old piece so it doesn't show from the inside. See **DIAGRAM 4.** When there are approximately 9 rows and the shape is established, lift the basket from the table and hold it with the ends of the stakes pointing away from you. Continue to weave in pattern. Just removing the basket from the table will allow the stakes to stand. You must determine how fast you want them to stand by the amount of tension you place on the weaver and stakes. Watch the space between stakes. If the spaces remain equal, the sides will be going up straight. If you see they are decreasing, that means the stakes are going in too much.

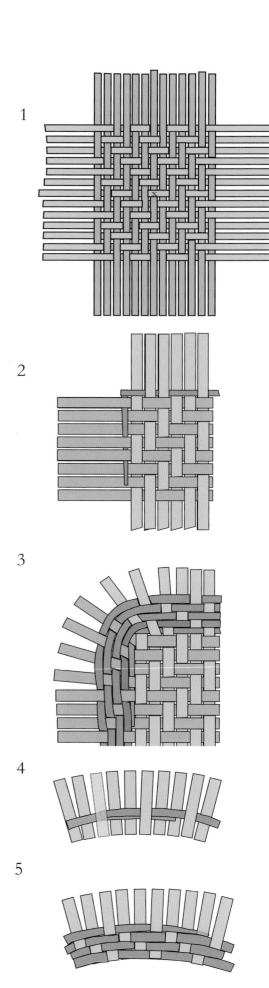

1

2

3

4

5

Now the real fun begins. Since there is no one way to accomplish this, I must give you very general instructions for creating the "Points of Light". **Staying in pattern** everywhere else, weave OVER or UNDER one, two, three or even four stakes (consistently) for four or five rows. Having struggled with wording this far too long, the following photos show you several examples I worked out for accomplishing the effect I wanted. You may find others. By all means, experiment with your own. Maybe you can show me some different ways I haven't thought of!

Weave in the o2, u1 pattern, making the points of light anywhere you want them, weave until the basket is 8"-9" high. Pack the rows tightly down every two or three rows.

Taper the end of the weaver for several inches and end it above the starting point to off set any unevenness you might have. See **DIAGRAM 5.**

Weave in a start-stop row of 3/8" heavy reed or ash as a false rim going over 2 and under 2. Dampen the ends of the stakes and bend the ones that are on the outside of the rim over to the inside and tuck them behind a row or two of weaving. Cut the stakes that are on the inside of the false rim flush with the top of the false rim.
See **DIAGRAMS 6 & 6A.**

MAKING THE PINE NEEDLE RIM:

If there is a secret to making a good pine needle rim, the first part is to have a good strong false rim row underneath. The second part is to keep the same number of needles all the time. Staggering them at irregular intervals is important so they begin and end singularly. See "Basket Class' for detailed instructions on rimming with pine needles.

Referring to **DIAGRAM 7,** hold approximately 30 needles, 15 on the inside and 15 on the outside. Tie the waxed linen on to the rim; thread the other end through the tapestry needle eye and lash around the needles, going into every space between stakes. If you opted to use a lasher, "hook" one end over the false rim and lash around the bundle, going through the spaces between stakes with the other end. Keep a close eye on the inside of the basket as it is hard to see the sewing needle coming through to the inside. Add a new needle every time an end is near. Place some if the ends on the left and some on the right. Even cut some off early (or readjust them) just so you can add new ones, one at a time. Push the new ends under the old ones or let the new one rest on top. The sheaths of the needles can stay on or be cut off later. If you need to, touch up the ends with black dye or permanent marker. Take care to shape the corners of the tray while you are putting on the rim. End the pine needles by pushing the ends under the beginning as in **DIAGRAM 8**. Cut some off anywhere it's needed. Just keep the ending area the same size as the rest of the rim. Back lash a few stakes (under the rim) to secure the end of the thread and cut.

These photographs will give you some ideas of the different results from just making changes in the weaving patterns.

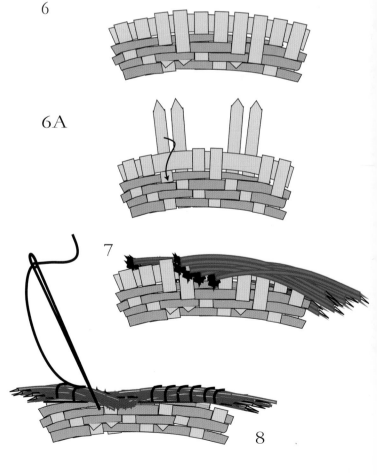

6

6A

7

8

81

Sante Fe Five

by Laura Lee Zanger

The Sante Fe Five undulating design was inspired by Laura's recollection of an Indian blanket she had as a child in the 1950's. The earth-tones adobe colors and the frequent use of 5/5 twill gives credence to the name. It is a challenge just to get all the dyeing done, but very "worth it" in the end. It's a really wonderful pattern and is only slightly indicative of the tremendously creative things Laura is doing. Enjoy !

Dimensions: 9 1/2" in diameter x 18" high including the handle

MATERIALS and PREPARATION

PRELIMINARY NOTES:

Choose flat reed that is true to size for the measurements to be accurate or adjust the lengths before cutting. Use the heavier, stiffer reed for stakes, and the more pliable for the weavers.

Various widths of the reed must be dyed. See Dyed Weavers.

Important: Stakes are measured in inches and weavers are measured by the foot.

MATERIALS:

1/4" flat reed natural for stakes,
    cut 60 pieces @ 32.5" for stakes
1/4" flat reed for weavers - about 22'
3/8" flat oval for rims
3/8" oval-oval (36" for handle)
#1 seagrass for rim filler on second rim
Razor blade knife with chisel blade for notching
    handle
#18 tapestry needle for lashing
Royal blue waxed linen

FORMULAS for mixing earth-toned adobe colors using RIT Dyes:

Dark terra cotta: Equal amounts Scarlet Red & Tan
Medium terra cotta: Equal amounts Scarlet Red & Taupe
Only dye for 5 minutes or until desired shade is reached
Desert Sand color: Taupe lightly dyed
Sky Blue: Evening Blue

DYED WEAVERS:

11/64" flat reed - dyed
    dark terra cotta - 12'
    medium terra cotta - 6'
    sky blue - 9'
1/4" flat reed - dyed
    dark terra cotta - 6'
    medium terra cotta - 6'
    desert sand - 12'
    sky blue - 12'
1/2" flat reed - dyed
    dark terra cotta - 6'
    medium terra cotta - 6'
    desert sand - 6'

BASE:

Soak all sixty 1/4" flat reed stakes in water for a few minutes. Divide them into two groups of thirty. Take one piece from each group and mark the rough side (wrong side) 12.5" from one end with an X. Lay one marked stake vertically on your work surface with the marked end nearest to you. Lay a spoke weight on top of it horizontally.

Now, lay the other stakes in that group to the right beside it with rough sides up, aligning the ends.

You will now weave in the other stakes horizontally, left to right, in a 3/3 twill. Start with the marked stake and weave U3, O3 etc., ending with an O3. The mark should line up with the other marked stake to form the lower left corner of the base as in **DIAGRAM 1.**

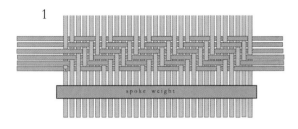

Align all the ends of the stakes with the marked one. Weave the first 6 rows in the following pattern:
Row 1: U3, O3, U3, O3, U3 etc. …end with O3
Row 2: O1, U3, O3, U3, O3 etc. …end with O2
Row 3: O2, U3, O3, U3, O3 etc …end with O1
Row 4: O3, U3, O3, U3, O3 etc …end with U3
Row 5: U1, O3, U3, O3, U3 etc … end with U2
Row 6: U2, O3, U3, O3, U3 etc … end with U1

Continue weaving the base upward by repeating these six rows, packing each row down tightly to the row before, to form a tightly woven herringbone twill base. Square the base and check your measurements. The base should measure approximately 7.5" x 7.5". Mark in pencil the corners and clip them with clothespins. **See DIAGRAM 2.**
Dampen all the stakes at the edge of the weaving. Bend the stakes all over upon themselves, toward the center of the

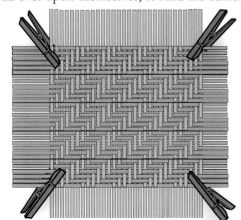

base. This is called "upsetting the stakes". Use a spoke weight at the edge of the weaving to help you bend at the right place.

WEAVING THE SIDES:

Weave the design with start-stop rows. See "Basket Class" for more detailed instructions.
Begin and end each row on a different side of the basket advancing one side each row.
Consult the graph on the next page (**DIAGRAM 3)** for the appropriate size and color of each row.
Note: Placing a spoke weight or ruler on each row of the graph, moving it upwards as you read the pattern, will help you keep your place.
Soak one dyed reed weaver at a time for only 30 seconds and wipe it 3 times with a towel to remove any excess dye before you start to weave. Slide each row down firmly and clip it in place. If your weavers have trouble staying down, you may be weaving too tightly, you may have made a mistake in the design, or the stakes may be too dry. Mist the stakes occasionally being careful not to soak the dyed weaver.
As you weave to the right, the stakes will have a tendency to lean to the right also. It is important to keep them straight and at a right angle to the weavers. Use a packing tool to help slide the stakes to the left. Pack down rows of weaving as you go. Use mini clips generously to help hold the rows in place and to hold the stakes upright as in **DIAGRAM 4.**

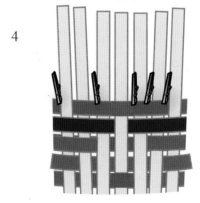

When you are finished weaving the design, 27 rows of pattern, you will weave one row in 1/4" natural. Mist the stakes. Do not wet the dyed rows. Make sure all stakes are standing straight and parallel. Pack down all rows of weaving.

3 - THE GRAPH

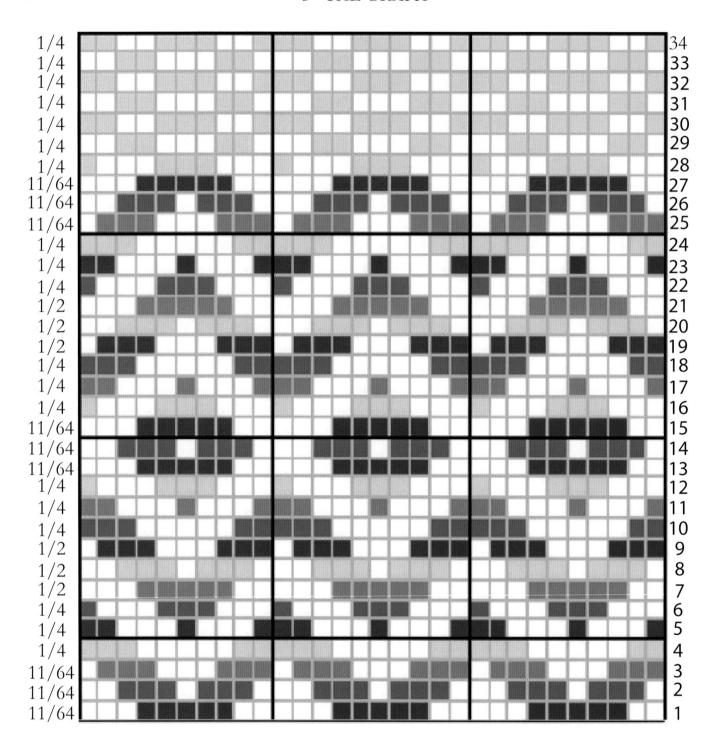

	Row
1/4	34
1/4	33
1/4	32
1/4	31
1/4	30
1/4	29
1/4	28
11/64	27
11/64	26
11/64	25
1/4	24
1/4	23
1/4	22
1/2	21
1/2	20
1/2	19
1/4	18
1/4	17
1/4	16
11/64	15
11/64	14
11/64	13
1/4	12
1/4	11
1/4	10
1/2	9
1/2	8
1/2	7
1/4	6
1/4	5
1/4	4
11/64	3
11/64	2
11/64	1

The 27 rows of pattern are undulated with varying widths of weavers. Rows 28-34 are woven with 1/4" flat reed weavers. Row 28 (first rim row) and row 34 (second rim row) are both covered with 3/8" flat oval rims. Follow the pattern carefully.

HANDLE PREPARATION:

Using the 36" piece of 3/8" oval-oval reed, measure and mark 7.5" from each end on the inside. Now take one piece of 3/8" flat oval reed (rim piece) to measure the width of the notch you will make. Measure towards the center of the oval-oval reed. Repeat this on the other end of the handle piece. Measure 1.25" toward the center and mark it again. Lay the 3/8" flat oval piece on the mark and draw another mark defining its width. Repeat on the other end as before. You should have four pairs of markings defining where to make the notches for the rims to fit onto the handle. Dampen the oval-oval reed before chiseling and shaping. With the chisel blade on your razor knife, position the blade on one of the marks and tap it into the oval-oval reed making a cut as shown. Move the blade to the left and right of the first cut and tap as before to make a consistent cut across the surface. Repeat this procedure on all of the marks. Using the unbeveled edge of the blade, carefully scoop out the 3/8" section. Be careful not to scoop too deeply. This works best by removing layers at a time. You do not want to thin the handle at those points where they might bend or crease. You are only notching it for the inside rim pieces to line up and hook up for rimming. See **DIAGRAM 5**. Shave the ends on the opposite side from the notches. These ends will be tucked into the weaving. Sand the handle. Smooth out any rough edges of the notching.

INSERT HANDLE:

Locate the center stake on two (opposite) sides of the basket where the handle will be inserted. Now cut off the three center stakes (one on each side of the center stake you just located) even with the top of the last row of weaving as in **DIAGRAM 6**. Insert the tapered end of the handle on the inside of the basket behind rows 3 and 4, counting from the bottom; line up the notches for the first rim.

FIRST RIM:

Now take the two 3/8" flat oval reed rim pieces and measure them to fit inside and outside of the last row of weaving. Taper the ends to overlap. Pin in place and then replace the clothespins with small cable ties. Lash with waxed linen beginning at the handle which encompasses 3 spokes. Cut away the cable ties as you lash. See **DIAGRAMS 7** and **8**. You will lash alternating between 3 and 2 stakes going all the way around the rim. Tie off the lashing when you get to the beginning. Start on the other side and reverse the direction of the lashing to make "X's" as shown. Tie off the lashing when you get to the beginning again. The 3-2-3-2 lashing will help you when weaving the next step.

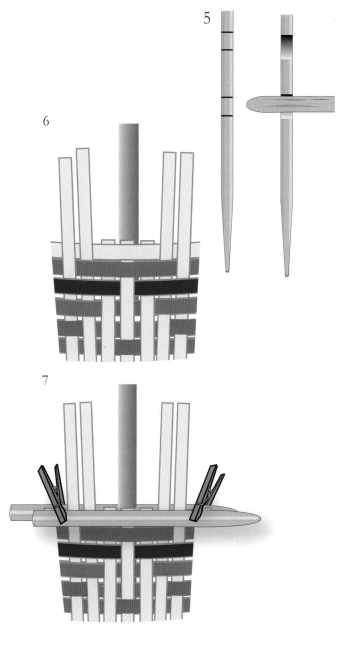

5

6

7

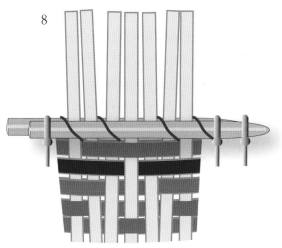

8

PLAITED SECTION:

Starting with row 29, using 1/4" flat oval reed, weave 6 rows of over and under in alternating groups of 2's and 3's (as if they were one stake) beginning over a pair. Weave around the stakes to overlap each other in their pairs and trios in a uniform manner. See **DIAGRAM 9.**

Cut the inside stakes (trios) even with the last row of weaving. Cut away one stake from each pair grouping. It is less bulky to cut the outside stake and trim and tuck the one nearest the inside of the basket. Soak the stakes for a few minutes. Bend them to the inside and tuck the ends behind a couple of rows of weaving.

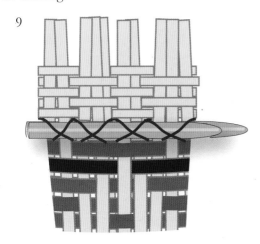

SECOND RIM:

Measure the 3/8" flat oval for the inside and outside rims. Cut them to fit and taper the ends to overlap. Pin in place using seagrass for the rim filler. Lash as before with waxed linen in one direction and reverse to get the desired "X's" on the rim. See **DIAGRAMS 10 AND 12.**

Allow the basket to dry. Trim any "hairs" or loose ends; oil and/or stain.

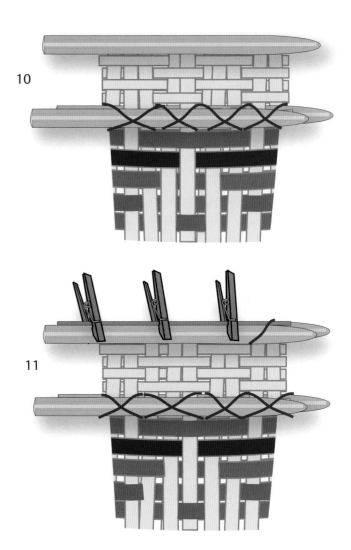

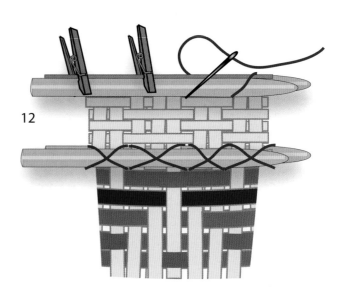

Inside View of
Rims and Handle

South of the Border

by Judy K. Wilson

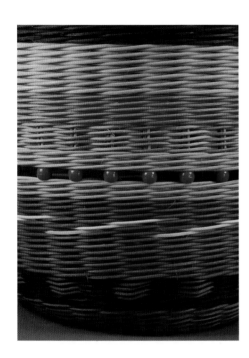

Dimensions: 7 ¾" high x 9" wide

Judy K. Wilson, of waxed linen fame, can still make reed baskets . . . and here's proof. Many years ago she made a small urn shaped reed basket for *Handmade Baskets* that was only pictured in the book. Well, here it is . . .and what a joy! Judy's very special, Spirit given gift of creating extraordinary color combinations is as apparent here as it was in those spectacular "Buttocks" Baskets in the 80's and 90's. There seems no end to the depth and breadth of her talent.

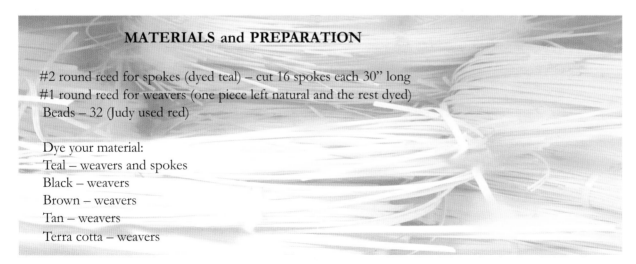

MATERIALS and PREPARATION

#2 round reed for spokes (dyed teal) – cut 16 spokes each 30" long
#1 round reed for weavers (one piece left natural and the rest dyed)
Beads – 32 (Judy used red)

Dye your material:
Teal – weavers and spokes
Black – weavers
Brown – weavers
Tan – weavers
Terra cotta – weavers

South of the Border is made completely with round reed. Different colors can be used for a different look. You can make this basket in any size reed, but the spoke length would have to be adjusted to accommodate larger sizes.
NOTE: Soak the weavers for only a minute or two in warm to hot water. Keep the woven portion of your basket lightly sprayed with warm water, especially the spokes so they will not break.

WEAVING THE BASE:

Soak a long teal weaver – the longer the better, uncoiled, in warm water for a minute or two. At the same time soak the 16 dark teal spokes for about one minute. Lay all the spokes on a table where you can basically see where the centers of the spokes are. Pick up four spokes, laying them side by side in your hand and hold them at the center point. Place them at the 12 o'clock /6 o'clock position. Pick up four more spokes (again laying them side by side), and stacking from the bottom, at the 9 o'clock /3 o'clock position. Pick up four more spokes and place them on the bottom, at the 10 o'clock /4 o'clock position. Pick up the last group and place them on the bottom, at the 2 o'clock/8 o'clock position. Hold all the spokes in place and gently lay them on the table (continuing to hold them in place). Clothespins on the ends help hold everything in place. The 12 o'clock group should be perpendicular to the 9 o'clock group. See **DIAGRAM 1.**

Leave all the spokes in place on a table.
As in **DIAGRAM 2**, pick up the long teal weaver. Go underneath the 2 o'clock group, placing the tail on top of the 12 o'clock group.
Hold in place with the left thumb. Go over the 3 o'clock group, under the 4 o'clock group, over the 6 o'clock group, under the 8, over the 9, under the 10 – and now you should be back at home (the 12 o'clock) position, where you started. Repeat this same pattern for a total of three times. Once all the spokes are caught in place, you may "spin" the spokes as you weave.

When you reach the 2 o'clock group again, divide only this group into two pairs this one time. See **DIAGRAM 3.** On the next row you will bring them back together as four. This changes the weaving path, reversing the overs and unders. Now go under 3 o'clock, over the 4:00, under the 6:00, over the 8:00, under the 9:00, over the 10:00 and under the 12:00. Repeat this for a total of three revolutions. Now, when you are back to the 3:00 group, divide this group into pairs only on this row. This again changes the weaving path and matches the first set of weaving. Again weave three complete revolutions, stopping where you began. There should be three sets of weaving with three rows each. See **DIAGRAM 4.**

Here you will introduce another teal weaver. Split the group where you are, placing the weaver, with the tail to the left, in between the two pairs of spokes. Begin to twine, dividing each and every group into pairs. See "Basket Class" for more detailed instructions on twining. Twine a total of three rows, stopping at home. The base should be in a circle and the stakes evenly spaced. See **DIAGRAM 5.**

Now you will introduce a third teal weaver and do 5 rows of "triple twine". Place the new weaver to the right of the existing weavers, in the next "slot" to the right. Hold in place until it is caught with the left hand. To triple twine, pick up the far left weaver each stroke, take it to the right, over 2 (sets) and under 1. Continue to always pick up the far left weaver. See **DIAGRAM 6.**

NOTE: When a weaver runs out, it should be on the right, with the other two weavers on the left of it. Tuck the old end into the weaving on the left side of the spoke after the spoke where it weaves behind. Crimp and push the new weaver into the weaving on the right side of the spoke you just went behind. For clarity, the weaver is shown in "natural" in the photograph.

Resume weaving again. **See DIAGRAM 7.** See "Basket Class" for more detailed instructions of how to add a weaver.

STARTING TO GO UP THE SIDES:

At home, you will now divide all the pairs of spokes into ones. If it seems "too tight", back up and triple twine another row or two over pairs. Then divide into "ones". At this point, pick the basket up off the table and hold it in front of you. Do not turn the base over. You are now weaving from the outside, up the sides of the basket. Just lifting the basket from the table causes the spokes to start to point upward.

Triple twine for a total of eleven rows over single spokes with the last five rows gradually turning up. Stop at home.

At home, you will be replacing all three weavers, but they must be cut and replaced one by one. Add three black weavers in the following manner.: Cut the farthest right weaver 1/2" past the spoke. Place a black weaver behind the same spoke and hold. Now weave the next teal weaver into place. Again, cut it ½' past the spoke it went behind. Place the second black weaver in place behind the same spoke. Repeat with the third weaver. Hold all the ends in place with your left hand. Begin to triple twine again for a total of two rows. Stop at home.

Hereafter, note that the following abbreviations will be used:

TT . . . triple twine

TW . . . twine

All the techniques have been explained. Look back for explanations.

At home, cut the weaver on the right when it is behind its proper spoke. Weave the next weaver into place. Cut it just past the next spoke and replace the weaver with brown. Now you have a brown and a black weaver. TW with the brown and black weavers for a total of four rows, stopping at home.

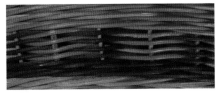

TW with black and brown

At home, with the black weaver on the right, replace weaver with a brown weaver. Then add another brown weaver to the right and TT for a total of seven rows. Stop at home. At home with the black on the right, replace weaver with natural and TT for three rows. The natural will automatically swirl if there are no mistakes.

Natural swirls

At home with the natural weaver on the right, replace weaver with brown and TT three additional rows above the natural swirls. See photograph above. Stop at home.

At home, replace each of the three brown weavers with tan (as explained previously) and TT for three rows.

Beads in place

At home, without cutting, place one pony bead on each of the spokes. The best method seems to be to place 8 – 10 beads, then TT to that point, place more beads etc. TT a total of three rows of tan above the beads. Stop at home.

Twine and cut as you did before with the previous black weavers, replacing the second tan weaver with terra cotta. Now, TW a total of five rows of tan and terra cotta. At home, replace the tan weaver (with it on the right) with terra cotta.

Then place another (3rd) terra cotta in the next right slot and TT five rows. Stop at home. You should have about 2" of weaving above the beads.

DOUBLE SPOKING :

Spray the upper part of the basket and using an ice pick or long awl, make an opening beside each spoke. On either side, right or left of the spoke, to give the top of the basket necessary strength, you will double the remainder of the spokes. Cut one end of a long piece of dry spoke material at an angle and insert the end of it into the weaving where you have opened the space. It won't go any farther than the bead. Cut the other end level with the top of the original spoke. See **DIAGRAM TO RIGHT.** Repeat this procedure with each spoke.

At home, you will replace all of the terra cotta weavers with teal weavers and TT seven rows, stopping at home.

At home, replace all three teal weavers with black weavers and TT nine rows. Stop at home.

MAKING THE BRAIDED EDGE:

Wet the spokes and the last inch of weaving. Hold your hand behind five or six spokes at a time and spray. You will be working to the right. It's important to keep the spokes side by side in pairs and to work them in snugly as you weave rather than trying to pull them tight at the end. The double spokes are treated as A SPOKE from now on. Pick up any spoke (called #1). Take it in front of the next spoke to the right (#2) and to the inside, behind spoke #3 and back to the outside. Pick up spoke #2. Take it in front of spoke #3, behind #4 and out. Repeat until you have two spokes left. Pick up spokes on the left and come in front of the spoke on the right and hold. Take an awl and slightly open up the hole underneath the #1 spoke. From the **back** come through the hole to the front and hold in place. Pick up the last spoke, go from **front to back** through the **very same hole**. Now you should be inside the basket. Look "next door to the right" and open up the hole with your awl under spoke #2 and go through it from the inside of the basket to the outside. Your first row of braiding is now complete.

Lightly spray the spokes again in front of the first braid so that they are soft. Note: spoke refers to pairs of spokes. Working to the right, pick up any spoke - #1 - go over the next spoke - #2 -, then lift the 3rd spoke. Take the spoke and go through the hole - to the far right - to the inside of the basket. Now pick up spoke #2, go over spoke #3 spoke, lift spoke #4, then go through the hole with the spoke. Repeat until you are down to two spokes. Take spoke on left, go over spoke on the right, open the hole slightly - with an awl- under the very first spoke (of the second braid), then go

through it to the inside of the basket and snug it up. Take the last spoke, go over the existing braid that comes next, then just past the next spoke, go through the hole to the inside of the basket. Tighten everything. Notice that the spokes are swirling to the right. Place your scissors at that same angle and cut all the ends just as they go behind the spoke on the inside of the basket.

Trim any "hairs" that might be on the outside of the basket. Your "South of the Border" is finished and ready for you to enjoy!

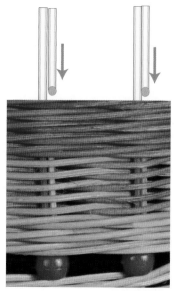

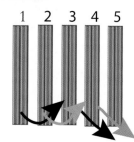

Drawings and Detail
Photographs
of Braided Border

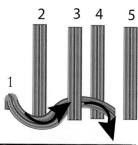

Spiral Staircase

by JoAnn Kelly Catsos

This charming basket woven of finely prepared Black Ash was inspired by the spindles of a graceful, winding wooden staircase. It has a twilled base, darker stakes and white weavers on the twilled sides, with lashed maple rims and handle.

Spiral Staircase is woven on a wooden mold and measures 4 1/4" in diameter at the rim and is 4 1/4" deep including the handle

MATERIALS and PREPARATION

Black Ash Splint (All materials available from Berkshire Splint, see Facts About Contributors)
    Stakes…from 1/8" ash, cut 30 @ 9"
    Weavers…from 3/32" ash, you will need approximately 25' (white color)
    Lasher…1/16" x 6' (white color)
    False rim… 3/16" x 16" (piece that is woven in and is covered by the rim)
    Rims… 3/16" hardwood rims
    Handle…1/4" wide hoop handle
4" mushroom mold, weaving stand and post
"C" clamp
Scissors
Small packing tool
Water bowl, ruler, pencil, one rubber band, four stainless steel pushpins
12 alligator clips, wood scraper with straight blade, sandpaper, Danish oil

THINGS YOU NEED TO KNOW ABOUT ASH:

1. Pieces of ash are referred to as "splints".
2. Sometimes there is no right or wrong side on a piece of splint. If there is a "rougher" side, call it the wrong side.
3. Dry splint will scrape or sand better than wet splint.
4. Damp splint will cut more accurately than dry. Before tapering with scissors, dampen the splint slightly.
5. With a pencil, lightly mark the center of each stake (on the wrong side…if there is one).
6. Dip the bundle of weavers into water for several minutes, uncoil, straighten and hang to dry.
7. Identify the right and wrong side of each weaver. Place a pencil mark on the wrong side (if there is one) several inches from one end.
8. Ash splint needs to be damp to be flexible but should never be soaked in water, unless otherwise noted. Use your fingers to transfer small amounts of water to the splint if needed to make it stay in place.
9. Use as little water as possible on the weavers. When dampened, the weavers will absorb water and swell in width. Later when the weavers dry, they will shrink in width and the weaving will suddenly become loose.
10. All baskets must be dried at certain points in the basketmaking process. Baskets may be air-dried which may take several hours, or they may be dried in the oven. To dry in the oven, preheat the oven at the lowest setting, then turn to **"off"**. Place the basket in the warm oven for 10-15 minutes until dry.

WEAVING THE BASE:

It is helpful to use a "loom" to hold the vertical stakes when weaving a base with many stakes instead of using a spoke weight to hold them in place.

To create a loom:

Lay three stakes, spaced ¼" apart, horizontally in front of

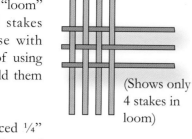

1

(Shows only 4 stakes in loom)

you. The loom is temporary and can be removed once the base pieces are stationary. Weave the ends of the 15 dry stakes with the "bad" side up, vertically into the loom in plain weave, Over 1, Under 1. Leave 1/8" spaces between the stakes. See **DIAGRAM 1.**

Now weave in the 15 dry stakes horizontally in a 2/2 twill, centering the first stake on the center of the vertical stakes. Weave over 2/under 2 (stepping the o2's over one stake each row). Leave 1/8" space between the stakes until all the stakes are woven and the 15 piece x 15 piece twill base is finished. See "Basket Class" for how to do a twill. Remove the three pieces that formed the "loom". The woven base should be centered. Check to be sure it is. If it is not, move the base weaving until it is centered. Pack the dry base stakes tightly together. Remember, it is more important that the base be square than tight. Pack stakes gently and as dry as possible, as dry stakes will slide easier than damp ones. If the stakes refuse to stay where they were packed, use your fingertip to place drops of water on the corners of the woven square. This will swell the "fibers" in the ash and make them "stay put".

UPSETTING AND WEAVING THE SIDES:

Dampen the stakes at the edge of the woven base and wait 1-2 minutes to allow the water to be absorbed into the splint. With the wrong side of the base facing up, upsett 6 stakes on each corner of the basket (3 on one side and 3 on the adjacent side) by creasing the stake back upon itself at the edge of the woven base. If the splint cracks, dampen it again and wait another minute before continuing. Ash splint has memory and the stakes will stand up slightly. See **DIAGRAM 2.**

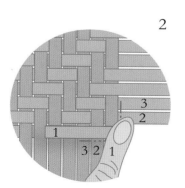

2

Turn the base over and place it on the center of the mold. If the mold has an "X" marked in pencil, with the two lines at right angles and intersecting at the center of the mold, this will help center the base. Pin the basket to the center of the mushroom mold with four pushpins. Gently open up little spaces between the stakes for the pins (three stakes in from each corner). Do not pin through the ash.

See **DIAGRAM 3.**

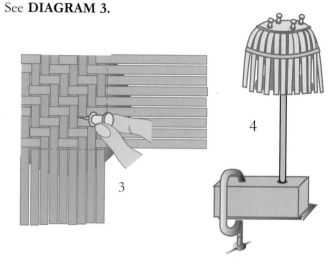

3

4

Secure the weaving stand to the table with the "C" clamp. Place the mold on the weaving stand and secure the stakes with a rubber band. See **DIAGRAM 4.**

Cut the stakes off 1" below the bottom of the mold. Adjust the spacing between the stakes.

STARTING TO WEAVE:

Choose the longest and lightest weaver that you have. Check the entire length for any flaws and sand if necessary. While dry, use a wood scraper to reduce the thickness of this weaver, first scraping ½" and then 1" back from the end of the weaver. Your goal is to remove about half of the thickness. Taper the other end to a fine point for about 2".

NOTE: Thinning the ends of all other weavers will help avoid bulges where two weavers overlap on the basket.

Dip this first weaver in water. The basket is woven in a continuous weave in a clockwise direction. The twill pattern is under 3, over 2, as in **DIAGRAM 5.** Begin with the tapered end of the weaver. Place it under three stakes on the far left of the basket side farthest away. Leave ½" of the tapered tail protruding from this corner.

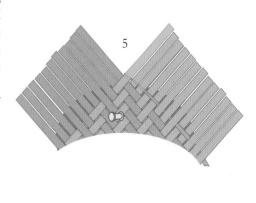

5

This will serve as a marker for the beginning stake.
THE TWILL PATTERN ON THE SIDES OF THE BASKET IS INDEPENDENT OF THE BASE TWILL.

The first row of weaving may "shadow" or be the same as part of the base weave.

When you have woven once around the basket and returned to the "tail" (beginning stake), you will have to make an adjustment in the twill so it will step over one stake to the right. That adjustment is "OVER 3 stakes" instead of "OVER 2". You will make this adjustment once in every row, at the end of the row. The "over 3" will spiral to the right up the side of the basket just like all the other O2 spirals.
See **DIAGRAM 6.**

6

OVER 3 spiral

Remember to use as little water as possible.

After three or four rows of weaving, fan the stakes so that the spacing between them is more even. Do this by scratching against the mold to drag the stake with your fingernail or packing tool.

Identify (and mark the ends with a pencil) the four pairs of stakes at each corner of the base. Each pair is made of one stake from the adjacent sides of the basket. Keep these pairs vertical, as two will be the location of your handle.

Weave against the mold and keep the rows snugly packed.

> Add a new weaver as needed by stopping the old weaver on top of an "over 2". Holding the new piece like dental floss, gently slide the new weaver in place on top of the old one, and weave with the two pieces for 4 sets of stakes. Cut the old weaver so it hides behind a stake. See "Basket Class" for details on adding a new weaver.

Continue weaving up to the top of the mold, continually adjusting the stakes so that they are vertical and the spacing is even. Dry the basket on the mold. The basket will shrink in height. Taper the end of the weaver to "almost threadlike" for 1 ½" past the beginning stake so the top of the basket is level. End the weaver behind a stake. See **DIAGRAM 7 .**

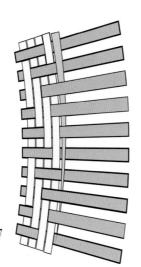

7

RIMS:

Dampen the false rim (a piece of 3/16" ash) and weave one separate row, exactly opposite the top row of weaving.
See **DIAGRAM 8.**

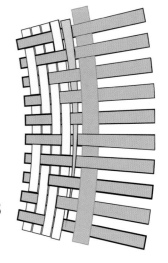

8

Remove the basket from the mold. Check the basket to be sure it is level. Repack the weaving below any "high" spots. Dampen the tips of the stakes without wetting the rest of the basket by holding the basket upside down and allowing the excess water to drip off.

Finish the top edge of the basket by crisply folding one of each group of the outside stakes (the stakes that pass on the outside of the false rim) over the false rim to the inside of the basket. If the splint cracks, dampen it again and wait a minute. Secure each fold with an alligator clip and dry for 5-10 minutes.

Cut the stakes that are still standing off flush with the top edge of the basket. See **DIAGRAM 9.**

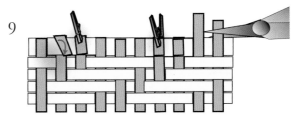

9

View from the Inside

Trim each folded stake so that it does not protrude past the bottom edge of the false rim.

Lightly sand the top edge of the basket with sandpaper to remove roughness.

93

Photo Detail
of Handle
and Rims

11

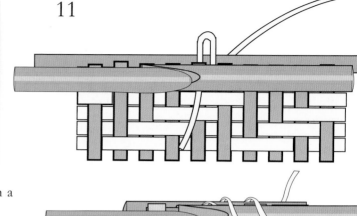

Test fit the handle and rims. Mark the rim overlaps with a pencil and adjust the scarf joint, if needed.

Notch the handle, removing a triangle shaped slice, that the rim will rest on, as in **DIAGRAM 10.**

10

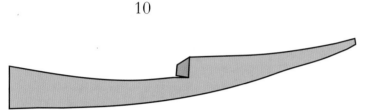

Finish sanding the rims and handle and apply Danish oil, letting them dry for about five minutes.

Carefully insert the handle inside the basket along the two adjacent corner stakes in two opposite corners. Start inserting the handle into the weaving about 1" down from the rim. Make sure the bottom of the notch lines up with the bottom edge of the false rim.

See "Photo Detail" above.

Fasten on the inner and outer rims using wooden clothes-pins or cable ties to hold them in place. The rims should overlap in a counterclockwise direction as you look down into the basket. (Clockwise for left-handed weavers) The rims should completely cover the false rim.

LASHING:

The rim of the basket will be single lashed. Begin with a lasher (lighter piece of 1/16" ash) that has been soaked for five minutes. Looking down into the basket, lashing will begin one stake past the outside rim overlap and progress counter clockwise (clockwise for lefties).

Place one end of the lasher, good side up, over the top rim with 2" of lasher protruding into the basket. Bend 1" on the end of the lasher forming a fish hook. With the hook, catch the inner rim of the basket between two stakes.

See **DIAGRAM 11.**

Using a packing tool to open up a space for the lasher, bring the short tip of the lasher over the false rim and back down between the false rim and the outer rim. Pull snugly. Lash around the top edge of the basket, to the right, stitching from the outside to the inside.

Make a neat X at each handle. When the lashing is complete, bury the tail of the lasher by bringing it up beneath the outer rim over the false rim and down under the inside rim. Trim the lasher tails. Your Spiral Staircase Basket is now finished. Sign and date your basket!

Spiraling Double Wall

By Lyn Syler

This fantastic double wall basket showcases the wonder of continuous weave; changing from one weaver to two, to three and then reversing the direction of the spiral by simply making a "mistake". Students marvel at the classic shape they are able to form by weaving the outside wall using the inside wall as a mold. Keiko Takeda's basket, "Tsubo," a marvelous example of the art of basketweaving (featured on the cover of Shereen LaPlantz's book, *Twill Basketry*), was my inspiration for Spiraling Double Wall.

Dimensions: Base 6" x 6"   Height 14"

MATERIALS and PREPARATION

5/8" flat reed (for stakes for inside wall)
3/8" flat reed (for weavers for inside wall)
7mm flat or flat oval reed - natural (for inside wall weavers and outside wall stakes)
11/64" flat oval - natural - (for outside wall weavers and lashing)
5/8" flat oval reed (rim)
Seagrass (rim filler)

Dye approximately 34 yards of 7mm flat oval reed the color of your choice
Then cut:
      7mm flat oval (dyed) 28 pieces 42" long
      5/8" flat reed (natural) 14 pieces 42" long

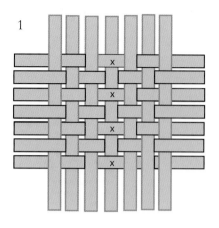

THE BASE:

Dampen the 5/8" flat pieces and mark the centers on the wrong side. Lay 7 pieces horizontally, wrong side up aligning center marks with approximately 3/8" between stakes. Weave the other 7 pieces in vertically, again aligning center marks in "Plain Weave". See **DIAGRAM 1.**

Insert two dyed 7mm stakes on top of each of the 5/8" stakes. Weave these in right side up (the 5/8" stakes and 7mm pieces will have their wrong sides together). NOTE: If this is difficult to do, "unweave" enough of the base to get the new stakes woven in on top of the others. The added thickness will cause you to have a little more space between the stakes. With all the stakes in, the base should measure approximately. 6 ½" x 6 ½". The base should resemble **DIAGRAM 2.**

STARTING THE WEAVERS:

Weave one start stop row of 11/64" flat reed around the base, mitering the corners to hold everything in place. See **DIAGRAM 3.** Overlap the ends for 4 stakes.

At this point, things get tricky. You have all the 7mm stakes to deal with while you are weaving the inner wall of the basket. The best thing I have found to do is put a rubber band around the 7mm stakes, making them look something like a giant pineapple. Now just try to ignore them.

Before you can start weaving, you must split one corner stake lengthwise, as shown in **DIAGRAM 4.**

WEAVING THE INSIDE WALL:

Taper the end of a soaked 7mm flat oval weaver for about 4" to almost 1/8" at the end. Start the "skinny" end, oval side down, at the split stake (see **DIAGRAM 4**) going over or under as the base weaving dictates and weave over 1 under 1. The odd (split) stake enables you to weave continuously as opposed to weaving start-stop rows. When the starting point is reached, simply continue as the weaving will automatically fall into the alternate path. Tapering the weaver offsets any "one-sided-ness" you would encounter in continuous weaving.

Keep the base flat on the table and continue to weave several rounds. While you are weaving the first several rounds, you must do two things:

(1) "Starburst" or " Fan" the stakes as in **DIAGRAM 5**; push them outward, away from the center sides, towards the corners. By the end of the 4th row, the large spaces at the corners should be filled in with stakes and they should all be about the same distance apart.

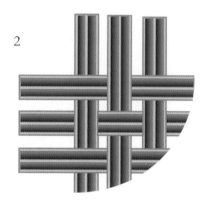

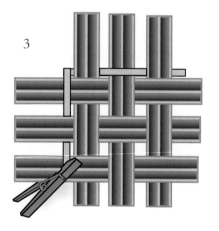

(2) Pinch the two corner stakes together and lift the corner off the table. As you are holding the corner stakes up and together, pull firmly on the weaver to keep them in place. This action is forming the "feet" or peaks on which the basket will sit. See "Basket Class" for this technique. You must repeat the procedure every row at every corner for several rows before everything stays in place.

Weave 6 or 7 rows (with 7mm weavers) with the base flat on the table. Then lift the basket from the table and continue weaving. Change the size of the weaver to 3/8" flat weaver after you have woven 14 rows total. Just lifting the basket off the table will cause the sides to go up, but don't allow them to go up too straight too quickly. After approximately 6" of weaving with the 3/8" weaver, start to pull tighter on the weaver and make the sides go straight up for about 10". See **DIAGRAM 6** for basic shape.

Pull even tighter on the weaver if you want the diameter of the basket to decrease at the top. Continue weaving to within 3" of the ends of the stakes. Taper the end of the weaver just as you began and end it directly above the starting point.

WEAVING THE OUTER WALL:

Remove the rubber band from the 7mm stakes and dampen the the stakes slightly. Press the stakes against the inner wall using it as a mold. See **DIAGRAM 7**. Keep the outer wall pressed tightly against the inner basket as the two must become one at the top. Begin weaving with a long damp piece of 11/64" flat oval reed, tapered at one end and weave continuously.

Begin weaving the following pattern: OVER 3, UNDER 1, OVER 2, UNDER 1, starting anywhere on the basket. This pattern will not change until halfway up the basket when you want to reverse the pattern direction. Weave approximately 15 rows in pattern with one weaver.

Then add another tapered weaver as in **DIAGRAM 8**, and weave with two weavers together for 8 rows, continuing in the same pattern. Then add a third weaver and continue in the pattern for 4 more rows, with the following change.

Now that you have three weavers, every time there is an OVER 3, take the center weaver under the center of the three stakes only, everything else is over all three stakes. See **DIAGRAM 9**.

REVERSING THE DIRECTION OF THE SPIRAL:

Now you must make an intentional "mistake" to reverse direction of the spiral. The "mistake" is OVER 4 instead of 3; then under 1, over 2, under 1 as usual. Return to the former pattern for the rest of the row. You will continue to make the "mistake" at the SAME place on EVERY row.

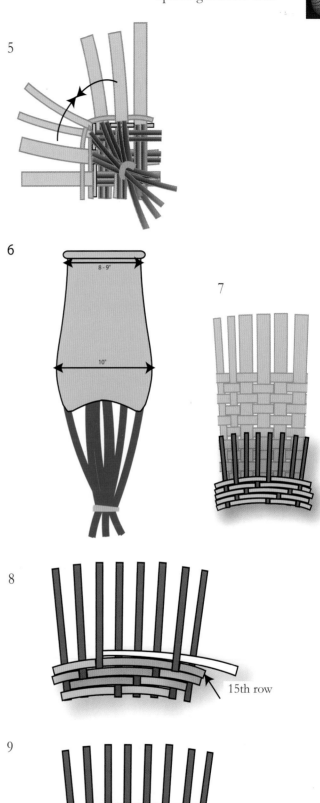

* center of three weavers

Weave 3 more rows with the direction reversed with 3 weavers. Taper the bottom weaver to a threadlike width and stop it behind a stake. Continue weaving with only two for 6 rows (or as many as you want) and then taper and stop the bottom weaver as before and finish the basket with one single weaver. Whether you reverse the direction of the pattern again is up to you; if you decide you want to reverse again, simply STOP making the "mistake". When the height of the outer wall is the same as that of the inner wall, taper the weaver as you began and end above the starting point. Weave a row of 3/8" flat reed as a false weaver; treating the two walls as one. Look for the split stake in the inner wall and treat it as one stake again so you can weave a start-stop row.
See **DIAGRAM 10.**

10

TIP: REMEMBER to always make the outer wall fit snugly against the inner wall using it as a mold. There must be no space between the two walls when you end at the top since they are woven together for the last row.

11

RIMMING THE BASKET:

Tuck the ends of the stakes into the weaving inside the basket. Tuck the inside stakes to the outside of the basket if you wish so the colored stakes don't show on the inside.

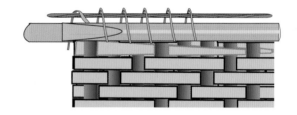

Measure the circumference of the top of the basket. Add about 4" for overlap; this measurement is for the outside rim. Cut the inside piece 2" shorter than the outside. Soak both pieces thoroughly. On both pieces, shave about half the thickness from the top of one end and the bottom of the other so the overlapped area is no thicker than a single thickness. See "Basket Class" for detailed instructions.

A Good View of the Spiraling Weave

Place both the overlaps on the same side of the basket, NEAR but not on top of each other. Make sure the ends are pointing in the same direction you are going to lash.
See **DIAGRAM 11.**

Place the rim filler on the top of and between the rim pieces. Hold everything in place with clothespins. Begin lashing just past (to the right if your are right handed) both the overlaps. Reverse everything, including the direction of the overlap, if you lash to the left. "Hook" the lasher over the basket wall, wrong side up, and bring it over the rim, right side up. Take the end into the next space under the seagrass filler and back down to the outside under the outside rim. Cut the ends flush with the bottom of the rim. Great job basketmakers; great basket!

Triple Diamonds

By Sosse Baker

Dimensions: 4 1/2" high x 3" square base

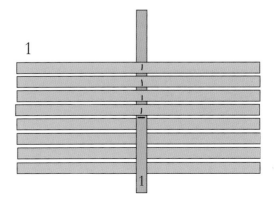

This double walled Chitimacha style basket begins with the elements diagonally plaited for the base. It continues diagonally up the inside, over and back down the outside, and is finished with a second base. When complete the basket is a beautifully formed vessel with a double base, double walls and no rim. "It is my intention to continue teaching this technique in an effort to promote the magnificent basketry of the Chitimachas". Sosse Baker, 2004

MATERIALS and PREPARATION

11/64" flat oval reed - select the most fine, most supple material
Cut 48 strands each 45" long
Dye color of your choice - Do not dye ahead of time, only when
instructed in the pattern

BASE:

Begin by marking the centers on eight spokes, laying those spokes out horizontally on a flat working surface. At the center marks weave one spoke perpendicular to the eight horizontal spokes, going over four spokes and under four spokes, starting from the bottom as in **DIAGRAM 1.**

1

Weave a second vertical spoke to the right of the #1 spoke, going under four and then over four. Then weave two more spokes vertically to the right of the center (#1) stake, and three more to the left of the center #1 stake, following **DIAGRAM 2** for the weaving pattern. This will give you an 8 spoke by 8 spoke center diamond pattern. Now, add four horizontal spokes both above and below the 8 original spokes, reversing the 4-3-2-1 order of over and under.. In the diamond base, the upper left set of four spokes starts over four and descends over 3-2-1 toward the center; therefore, you add the next horizontal spokes under 4-3-2-1, working from the center.. See **DIAGRAM 3**.

Next add four vertical spokes on each side, again reversing the 4-3-2-1 order of the preceding set of 4 verticals, over and under in the opposite order. Add one additional set of four spokes all around, reversing the preceding 4-3-2-1 order of over and under. The base is now complete with 24 spokes on each side. See **DIAGRAM 4**. The base will measure approximately 3" x 3".

3

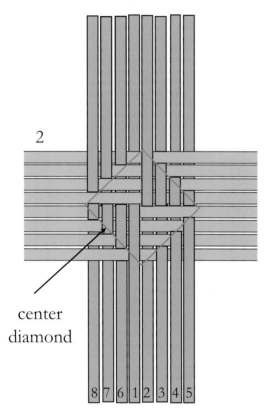

2

center
diamond

8 7 6 1 2 3 4 5

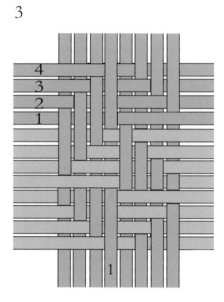

STARTING TO WEAVE THE SIDES:

Visually, "square the diamond" and fold the corner triangles outside the square upward. In diagonal weaving, the spokes become the weavers.

Now you will weave the corners. The smooth or oval side of the spokes will be on the inside as you weave, with the wrong (rough) side facing out.

DIAGONAL WEAVING:

"Turn the Key and Lock It" is a term taught to Judy Olney by Claude Medford. I'm quoting the following explanation from her book:

> "The key is the 12th spoke from the left on any side of the base. It is also the spoke just to the left of the center line. It has gone over four spokes. Turn the key so that it lies parallel to the base weaving on its right. Weave it going under 4, over 4, under 4, over 4. This weave is a continuation of the twill weave pattern established on the base."

See **DIAGRAM 5**.

4

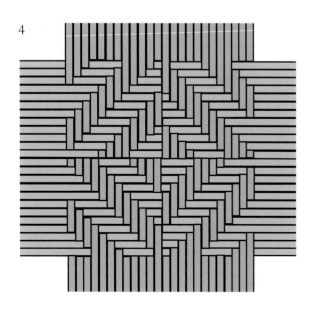

Completed base 24 spokes x 24 spokes

100

Once the key is locked on all four corners, the first couple of rows fall in to place diagonally. One set of spokes is inside and one set is outside. Each row brings the inside spokes out from behind four outside spokes. Weave up until six rows are completed.

As illustrated in **DIAGRAM 6**, cut off the 48 outside spokes, leaving a 1/8" tail. Dye the spokes that you have cut off. Then reinsert the dyed spokes over the cut off tails and down under four spokes to secure. See **DIAGRAM 7.**

Now all the spokes on the outside are dyed, and all the spokes on the inside are natural. Do one more round of sets of four, then switch to sets of two (instead of four) to tighten the new spokes in place. End with a dyed row on the outside. You will see this in **DIAGRAM 8.** Place a rubber band or tie a string around the top row to hold it in place.

WEAVING THE OUTSIDE WALL:

The next step is to weave over the top and down the OUTSIDE of the basket. Now, the double wall begins. Take two natural spokes and fold them down in an upside down V. Then bring one of the inside dyed spokes out and over the upside down V in the opposite direction.
See **DIAGRAM 9.**

Alternate single dyed and single natural spokes to complete the two-two twill around the top of the basket. Turn the basket over and continue diagonal weaving in sets of two for two rows. On the next row, with the natural side out, begin following the graph. Follow the graph pattern or return to weaving alternating rows down the outside weaving, until you are slightly higher than the inner bottom of the basket.

5

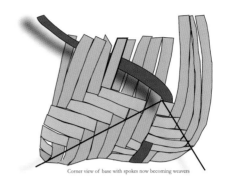

Corner view of base with spokes now becoming weavers

6

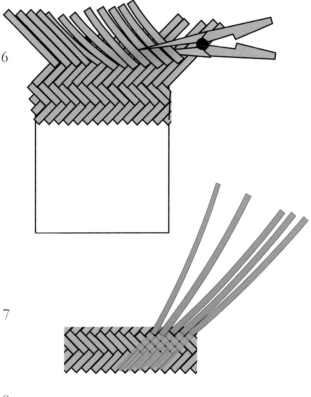

7

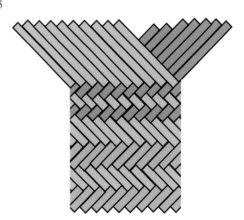

8

9

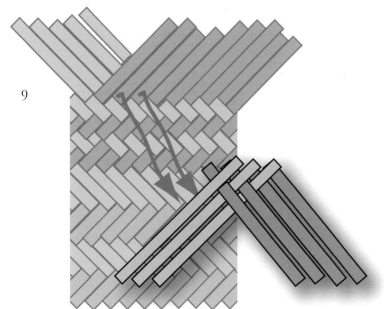

Graph for Outer Wall

Note: The basket has been turned upside down in these diagrams

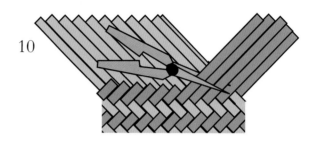

10

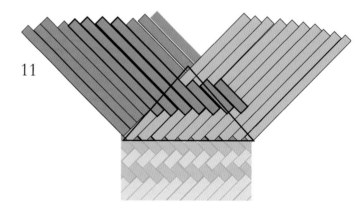

11

This is the side with both dyed and natural stakes remaining

12

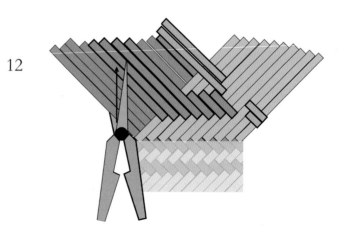

Now comes the most difficult part of the basket. I find that if I work a little at a time, it seems easier. These directions assume that you now have the natural spokes on the outside and the dyed spokes on the inside. One at a time, cut the inner dyed spokes off, on three sides, leaving ¼" tails. These tails will just lay underneath the base once the weaving is complete. See **DIAGRAM 10.**

Begin with the side that has both sets of spokes remaining. Folding them over, the natural spokes will be on top, heading to the right, while the dyed ones will be underneath heading to the left. See **DIAGRAM 11.**

Start weaving those outer spokes at the point of the triangle that is formed by the inner spokes, working into the side that is folded over to the center of the base. You will have your first triangle. The dyed spokes lying to the left side can be trimmed straight along the edge of the base, as they will be buried under the finished base. **See DIAGRAM 12.**

Rotate the basket to the right and weave the next side of outer natural spokes. Bring the corner natural spoke over the first set of four, then under four, and over four. Bring out the spoke that is lying down, out the side, then bring the next spoke that is standing up, over and across. See **DIAGRAM 13.** Finish out that side and rotate. Bring the natural spoke on the corner across the top of the triangle by going over the first set of four, then under four, over four, under four, over four, under four and out on the opposite corner; leave a tail. Bring the first natural spoke that is under the diagonal over four, (just woven across), out the side of the base. Now pick up the natural spoke on the edge and weave that all the way across, over four, under four, over three, under three (in the center) then over four and under four and out the other side.

Each time you get to that opposite side, bring the natural spoke that it comes out in front of, over, and tuck it in the base. Continue until all the spokes are woven in and you have tails out on three sides, and a set coming out in the second row of one side of the base. Dampen the whole base; then one at a time, pull each spoke tight and cut it off as close as you can. See **DIAGRAMS 14 and 15.**

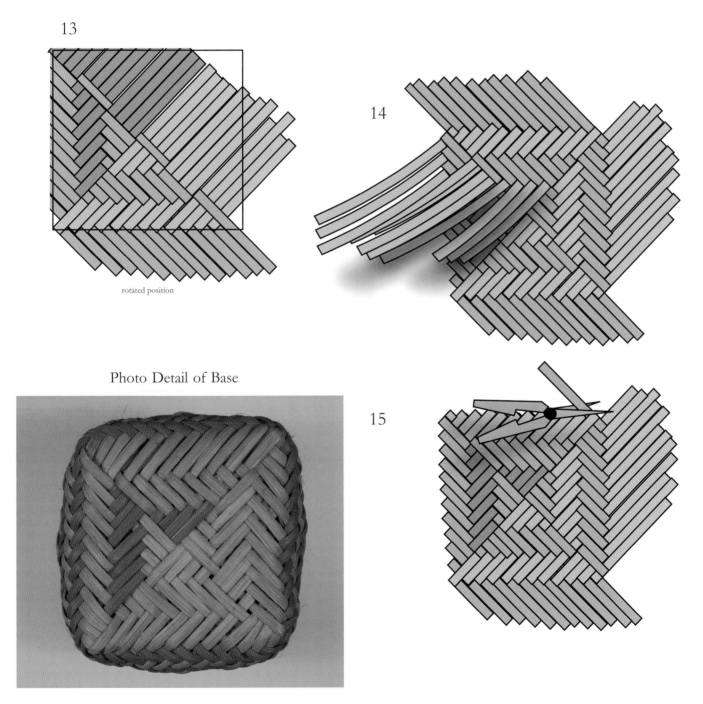

13

rotated position

14

Photo Detail of Base

15

Woven Watercolors

By Carolyn Kemp

Carolyn Kemp's love of watercolor and weaving combine in her artistic "Woven Watercolors". These instructions make it easy for anyone to create their own pendant, earrings or pin. Be experimental and try some variations of your own.

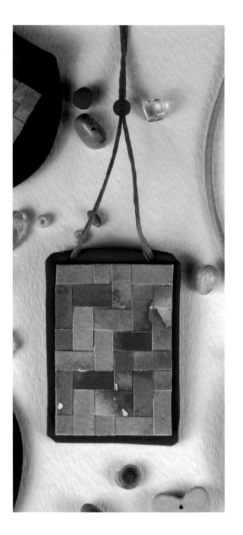

MATERIALS and PREPARATION

One sheet of 120 lb. watercolor paper (enough for numerous projects)
Watercolor or water based acrylic paint, colors of choice
One 2 ounce package of oven-bake clay, color of choice. I use a dark brown or black
Razor blade knife and metal straight edge (or pasta machine)
White glue and gel instant glue
Small piece of mat board or any heavy cardboard, to use as a weaving surface
Double faced cellophane tape
One wooden skewer, small (about the diameter of a toothpick)
Waxed linen or any cord of choice for the necklace
Medium size brush for painting paper (one from your child's paint set will work; don't go out and invest in camel hair watercolor brushes)

Cut two pieces of watercolor paper approximately 4" x 4" – one will be woven, one will be the backing
Select paint colors you like; this is entirely up to you, personal preferences dictate.
My colors are Payne's Gray, Burnt Sienna, Yellow Ochre and Phthalo Blue

PAINTING THE PAPER:

Paint your paper using the "wet" technique.

Dip your brush into a container of clean water, then dip the wet brush into paint, mixing the water and paint to a consistency of runny cream. Now just dab the paint on the paper; you are "applying" color, not painting a picture. Relax and have fun! See **DIAGRAM 1**. Rinse your brush in the other water container and select another paint color, butting one color up right against the other.

Let the wet paint mingle, merge, and run. I even pick the paper up, tilting it and letting my colors blend into one another. Keep adding colors until you fill the paper, and then let it dry; don't worry if it curls, you are going to cut it in strips. See **DIAGRAM 2**.

Once your painted paper is dry, turn it over and mark off your strips (weavers) with a pencil and ruler.
See **DIAGRAM 3**.

Each strip will be 3/16" – 1/4" wide and 4" long (there is lots of flexibility in the size of the strips; just be consistent in your choice; all the strips should be the same size). Also, if you have a pasta machine you can use it to cut your paper. Cut 24 pieces (enough for two pendants).

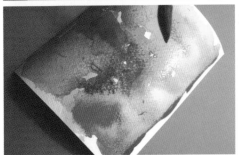

WEAVING YOUR PENDANT:

I found a shortcut that really makes weaving these small pieces easy. Take about 3" of double faced tape and stick it on the cardboard weaving board close to the edge. Pick any six to eight painted strips and lay the ends on top of the double faced tape, placing them parallel to each other with about 1/16" in between. The tape will hold the strips in place as you weave. See **DIAGRAM 4**.

You will do a two/two twill weave:

Row 1 - over 2, under 2 etc.

Row 2 – under 1, over 2, under 2 etc.

Weave 8 rows (or more, depending on the size and shape you like) in the twill pattern, over 2, under 2.

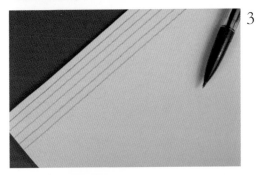

Remove the weaving from the tape and pack the rows tightly so that there are no spaces between the strips.

DIAGRAM 5 shows the weaving packed but not glued to back. Cut the second (backing sheet) of watercolor paper approximately the same size as the woven watercolor. You are going to the glue this piece to the woven watercolor.

Coat the back side of the woven watercolor with white glue, making sure the glue goes all the way to the ends of the weaving and is spread evenly. At this point your weaving has irregular edges, you will straighten them out later. Take the backing piece, spread a thin coating of white glue inside the marked area and press the two together. Your woven strips will still be moveable, so make any last minute adjustments at this time. If glue starts to seep out, wipe it off.

6

7

7A

8

After the glue is dry and you are sure that nothing will slip, take your razor blade knife and straight edge and cut through the double thickness of watercolor paper following the edges of the outermost weavers as your guide. See **DIAGRAM 6**.

PENDANT:

Kneed a piece of clay, making it soft and easy to shape. Roll the softened clay into a ball, making sure that there are no air pockets in the clay. Using your hand, or a smooth roller, flatten the ball into the desired shape. Sometimes it takes me many tries to get the shape and size I like. If you don't like it, roll it up again and start over. Once you get an oval, rectangle or whatever shape you like, take your woven watercolor and place it on the clay for final positioning. Do not press it in yet. Put some instant glue on the woven watercolor and now push it into the soft clay.
See **DIAGRAM 7**. Once the weaving is in place, you have the option to trim the clay with a kitchen knife or razor blade if you want to change the shape. See **DIAGRAM 7A**. Take an awl or a wooden skewer and make a hole large enough in diameter to put your necklace through. See **DIAGRAM 8**.

Bake the clay with the woven watercolor glued on, following the directions on the "oven-bake" clay. The low heat will not hurt the woven watercolor. Carefully remove the pendant from the oven and let cool. Attach it to your favorite necklace: use waxed linen, cotton cord, leather or even a pretty chain. Adding beads or other embellishments is a matter of personal taste.
"Wear your Woven Watercolor with the same pride and joy that I do....... and then make one for a friend." Carolyn Kemp

Carolyn loves combining different materials to create really unique jewelry!

Facts about the Contributors

(A glimpse into the personal "odysseys" of our talented guest basketmakers)

Sosse Baker - Chester, Connecticut

It is quite possible that Sosse Baker has given more to the basketmaking world than any other single person. A weaver for many years, Sosse's work has received recognition literally all over the world. In 1993 she spent the summer in Uganda, assisting Ugandan basketmakers in quality control for the US market. It was a life  altering experience for Sosse. With no instruction and only a broken basket, she figured out the techniques used for the Chitimacha double walls and continues to work with their patterns, making them in her own imaginative configurations. Sosse and Jack Baker are owners of the CHESTER GALLERY in Chester, CT. **Contact:** SosseJack@aol.com

Sherry Clayton Baldwin - Asheville, North Carolina

 A self-described "addicted knitter" for nearly fifty years, Sherry is also an avid hand-spinner and basketmaker. With a professional career as a counselor specializing in crisis/trauma, "Doc B," so called by her school-aged clients, finds that her hand crafts bring a welcome "hands-on" relief to the stresses of emotional and mental work. Sherry's current knitting passion is to design one-of-a-kind sweaters and knitted items from "the intention of my imagination". **Contact:** scbaldwin28704@yahoo.com

JoAnn Kelly Catsos - Ashley Falls, Massachusetts

JoAnn wove her first basket in 1985 and now she and her husband, Steve, harvest their own Black Ash materials and run their business, Berkshire Splint. JoAnn travels around the United States conducting basketmaking workshops and seminars.  Her work has been featured in *Splintwoven Basketry* by Robin Taylor Daugherty, Early American Life magazine, Shuttle, Spindle and Dyepot, Just Patterns, Basket Bits. In 1999 she wove an ornament for the White House Christmas tree. JoAnn's specialty is weaving miniature baskets which have won numerous awards. In 2003 she earned the Certificate of Excellence in Basketmaking from the Handweavers Guild of America. **Contact:** catsos@adelphia.net or write to her at 90 Polikoff Road, Ashley Falls, MA 01222

Faye Clause - Maggie Valley, North Carolina and Orange City, Florida

 Faye has been making baskets since the early 1980's. Her natural vine baskets are recognized by basket enthusiasts from many parts of the country, especially the east coast. She has taught for many years in North Carolina, Michigan, Tennessee and Florida; she has taught classes at John C. Campbell School in Brasstown, NC. Faye has used almost every natural material at one time or another but usually starts with two grapevine hoops. **Contact:** fayeclause@webtv.net

Anne Coleman - Danville, Kentucky

Anne Coleman sums up her life in just a few key words, "I am a professional artist who paints, works in clay, weaves and travels...and I'm smart and pretty!" Anne started making baskets in 1984, and we hope she never stops. It would be hard to find another basketmaker who comes up  with as many unique baskets as Anne does. If you want the horse pin used in Derby Day, **contact:** Anne Coleman, 705 Spears Lane, Danville KY 40422 (859) 236-7853

Debra Hammond - East Earl, Pennsylvania

 Debra Hammond lives in Lancaster County, Pennsylvania where she owns and operates a basket weaving studio and supply shop. She has been weaving baskets and teaching basketry since 1990. Debra teaches ongoing studio classes, 4-H classes and adult education classes at area high schools; she also travels and teaches at numerous state basket conventions and guild seminars. Debra's work in round reed and mold weaving is widely recognized. Her professional goal is to share her passion for weaving baskets and her expertise in the technical aspects of basket construction with others. **Contact:** 1709 Turkey Hill Road, East Earl PA 17519 email: thbasket93@yahoo.com

Patti Quinn Hill - Weaverville, North Carolina

Patti is a studio artist living in Weaverville, NC. Her contemporary style leans more to the artistic elements of design, working in hand painted, woven and embellished archival paper. She is a member of the Southern Highland Craft Guild and has been on their Board of Trustees. Her teaching experience consists of workshops at Penland School of Craft, Craft Summer at Miami University in Oxford, Ohio, Arrowmont School of Craft, Tennessee Arts Academy, and American Craft Council Southeast Seminar. She has been featured in books, galleries, museums and invitational shows. Patti's work is in many public and private collections and she has received awards for her baskets at gallery shows, fairs and national basketmaking conventions. Patti's work can be acquired through Blue Spiral I Gallery, the Folk Art Center, the del Mano Gallery, the Center for Southern Craft and Design and by commission. **Contact:** pattiquinnhill@charter.net or write to Patti at: 6 Jump Cove Road, Weaverville NC 28787 (828) 645-6633.

Facts about the Contributors

Gail Hutchinson - Milton, West Virginia

Gail divides her time between teaching basketry, designing new patterns and thinking "out of the box". She loves to break the rules and see where her imagination and experimentation will take her, "testing the materials to the max to see what they will do". Gail is on the artist advisory board for "TAMARACK...The Best of West Virginia" (if you have ever driven north or south on Interstate 77 through the middle of West Virginia, you probably have seen the interesting silhouette of this large juried craft center, home to more than 2000 West Virginia crafts people). **Contact:** Weaveme02@aol.com

Dianne Kennedy - Asheville, North Carolina

Dianne is a self taught basketmaker who designs baskets, writes

original patterns and teaches classes. "I have been teaching basketmaking for about 15 years and especially enjoy teaching beginners." Dianne has been involved with the NC Basketmakers Association as a convention co-coordinator, a board member and volunteer. In addition she has taught at several conventions and seminars east of the Mississippi and has been an instructor at John C. Campbell School at Brasstown, NC. Presently Dianne is membership chair for the Tennessee Basketry Association and is an at-large member of the NC Basketmakers Association.
Contact: www.bungalowebasics.com or
email:DianneC7@aol.com
230 Pennsylvania Ave., Asheville, NC 28806 (828) 285-0408

Eileen LaPorte - Washington, Michigan

Eileen has been involved with crafts all her life; knitting, cross stitch, quilting, weaving, macrame, etc. When she took her first basket class that was it. "There was something different about making a basket and I just needed to continue making baskets." Eileen is a former teacher so she was able to go on and continue her love of

teaching but this time teaching basketry. She has said all along that when basketmaking was no longer fun, she would stop. She has traveled to England, Germany and Australia several times with her basketry friends to explore other basketry events. She continues to teach basketry and does a couple of art fairs each summer. Basketry is still fun!
Contact: eileen_laporte@yahoo.com or write to her at:
8275-31 Mile Road, Washington, MI 48095-1302 (586) 752-2853

Dory Maier and Dianne Masi - Hampstead, North Carolina

Dory Maier grew up in New York State and was captivated by the Native American culture represented by the Seneca Nation from her region. "I wanted to learn their craft and to pursue pottery and basket making." Dianne Masi grew up in Connecticut and always had a love for arts and crafts; she has worked in many mediums. When Dory moved to North Carolina, she found a woman with whom she bartered pine needle lessons in exchange for weeding and pruning the woman's yard. Then Dory and Dianne met and their friendship and creativity have grown together. Dory says that Dianne "not only learned to coil, but embraced it with a degree of sophistication of a person born to the craft". Dianne feels that pine needle and gourd art will be her love for a long time. **Contact:** Dianne: dfree2bme@yahoo.com and Dory: dorymaier@yahoo.com

Wendy Reary - St. Louis, Missouri

Wendy has been the owner of St. Louis Basketry Supply since January 1995 and a basketmaker since the fall of 1991. "I weave for fun, obviously not for profit, just ask my husband, Dave." Wendy's enthusiasm for basketry is infectious; she has guided, as only Wendy can, countless beginners in the St. Louis area. Her talent is a gift to all of us. Her patterns and designs are truly inspiring!
Contact: www.stlbasketry.com email: stlbskt@juno.com or St. Louis Basketry Supply, Inc. 11420 Gravois Rd., St. Louis MO 63126, (314) 843-5005

Judy K. Wilson - Canton, Georgia

Judy has always loved small intricate crafts; even as a child she was creating and making things, so it is of little surprise that she should choose coiling/twining with waxed linen /silk to be her forte. Judy loves old Native American Baskets, their patterns and colors and has a passion for figuring them out and creating her own new ones. She has been making baskets since 1984 when she perfected the fabulously colored "buttocks baskets" in her north Georgia home, giving herself "something to do". Thankfully, she was listening the day her Source of Creative Energy spoke to her! **Contact:** email: windywindy1919@yahoo.com or visit her web site at www.judykwilson.com.

Laura Lee Zanger - Augusta, Georgia

Laura Lee Zanger began her weaving journey when a friend taught her to make a melon basket. Shortly after that first lesson her husband bought her first basketmaking materials including Lyn Siler's "How to Make Baskets" series. This was when she came to love and learn about basketry. Laura has a real passion for twills and Cherokee double weaves. "I feel that Lyn has been with me throughout my weaving journey and now I have come full circle with Lyn making note of my work." **Contact:** 2220 Lumpkin Road, Augusta GA 30906 (760) 560-9800 email - LLZanger@aol.com

Donating untold hours to our
"Quality Control"
Carolyn's dog, Tar Heel

GLOSSARY

Aging The process that occurs when a basket turns dark from natural environmental elements.

Arrow The rows of weaving that form an arrow pattern. Consists of one row of regular weave, a step-up, a reverse weave and ending.

Ash splints Strips of ash that are thinned enough to use for stakes or weavers.

Awl A tool resembling an ice pick used for opening spaces and making holes in reed. It is shorter than an ice pick and not as sharply pointed.

Base The bottom of the basket; woven mat.

Bevel To cut a square edge to a sloping edge; scarf.

Binder cane Cane that is wider than regular strand cane; used recently to lash basket rims in place.

Bi-spokes Extra or added spokes, inserted beside the original ones.

Bow-knot ear A four-point lashing ear, wrapped only once and "tied" in front.

Braided God's Eye A four-point lashing like the regular God's Eye except it is interwoven and appears braided to the eye; woven God's Eye.

Braided handle Any of several different methods of interweaving the reed around the handle; specifically, the wheat braid.

Brake A short piece of reed woven alternately above the beginning of a weaver to hold it in place.

Butt To bring the ends of any two pieces together, flush against each other.

Cable cast on A method of casting on stitches used in knitting when a stronger finished edge is desired and no ribbing is present.

Cane The outer peel of rattan, used in weaving, or as an embellishment, and on chair bottoms.

Chain pairing The same as pairing or twined arrows.

Chase weave A method of weaving with two weavers at once. Continuous weaving over an even number of stakes. The weaver moves first, and the chaser (the other weaver) follows alternately.

Coil One row of waling that ends with a step-up and a lock.

Coiling A weaving technique using an inner core which is wrapped solidly with a smaller thread.

Continuous weave Weaving done over an odd number of stakes. It is not done one row at a time, but rather continuously from beginning to end, with weavers added periodically.

D handle A basket handle that continues across the bottom of the basket and that, turned on its side, resembles the letter D.

Diagonal weave A method of weaving in which the elements interweave with themselves. Also called diagonal plaiting and oblique weaving.

Double-bottom A method of construction in which one base is woven and a second (woven) one is placed on top of the first.

Double wall A basket that either starts with a twill or plain weave double base and uses half the stakes to weave the inside wall and the other half to weave the outside wall. A rim holds the two walls together.

Double weave A Native American Basketmaking term that employs diagonal weaving, beginning and ending with a base. The basket has no added rim.

Dyeing Coloring reed with any number of natural or chemical dyes.

Ear (1) Weaving or lashing done at the intersection of the rim and handle that holds the two pieces securely. (2) Lashing into which the ribs are inserted. (3) Loops that join a swinging handle to the basket.

Embellishment Any decorative treatment done to the handle or body of the basket that is not essential to its construction.

Fanny The twin, gizzard-shaped bottom of an egg shaped basket; buttocks.

Filling in On some ribbed baskets a wedge-shaped area remains unwoven when the rim is full; it must be filled in by some type of "back and forth" weaving, also called packing.

Five-point lashing A lashing (ear) done around any five intersecting pieces.

Frame The support (usually wood) around which the basket is woven.

French randing A strong diagonal randing pattern that uses short rods (weavers) that are begun at the base one at a time.

God's Eye A four-point lashing; ear.

The Perfect God's Eye

Grapevine A vine used for weaving baskets and handles.

Hairs The splinters from the reed that usually occur from overuse, to be clipped or singed when the basket is finished.

Handle The part of the basket by which it is carried.

Honeysuckle A wild vine used for weaving baskets, smaller than grapevine.

Hoop Ring or piece of wood shaped into a circle; machine or handmade, present in ribbed baskets.

Indian weave A method of continuous weaving over an even number of stakes/spokes, adjusted each round by weaving over two spokes so the alternate over/under pattern resumes.

Japanese weave Weaving over two spokes and under one.

Lasher The piece of reed that wraps around and secures all the rim pieces together.

Lashing The act of wrapping all the rim pieces or wrapping the ear; the pieces of reed used to wrap are also referred to as lashing.

Loom Temporarily placed warp or weft stakes that hold the beginnings of a flat base in place when starting to weave.

Loop An ear that holds the swing handle and pushes down into the basket.

Losing a lasher "Lose" means to hide the end of the reed in the rim or in the weaving.

Mat The woven base of a flat basket.

Notch The indented space on a push-in handle made to fit under the rim and prevent the handle from pulling out.

Oak splints Strips of oak wood thinned enough to use as stakes or weavers; also called splits.

Oblique weave Diagonal plaiting or weaving.

Osier Any of various willows that have tough, flexible twigs or branches which are used for wicker work.

"Wicker Work" Original Drawing by Carolyn Kemp

Packing (1) Pushing each row snugly down beside the previously woven row. (2) A method of building up or filling in an area by turning one spoke sooner each row.

Pairing Twining

Plain weave Over-one, under-one weave; randing.

Plaited Woven.

Pre-formed Shaped or formed before being used.

Randing A simple over/under weaving with a single weaver and an odd number of stakes.

Rattan A climbing palm (vine) from which reed is made.

Reed The inner core of rattan that has been cut into either flat, round, flat oval, half round, or oval shapes; used for baskets and furniture.

Rib The round or oval pieces that extend from one side of the basket to the other and form the basic skeleton.

Aaron Yakim "Ribbed" Herb Basket

Rim The pieces, inside and outside, that fit over the top row of weaving to form an edge and give stability to the sides.

Rim filler A piece of round reed, seagrass or other suitable material that goes between and on top of the two rim pieces.

Scarf A joint in which the ends of any two pieces are cut so they overlap each other and join firmly.

Scarfing To join by cutting the two end pieces, usually beveled or on a slant, so they fit together smoothly.

Seagrass A twisted rope of grass suitable for weaving.

Shaver An instrument used for shaving away wood; a small rasp.

Sight To look at a basket frame and determine the rib lengths to give the desired shape; to eyeball.

Slewing A wicker work weave done with two or more paired weavers in a randing pattern.

Slype	A long, gradually slanted cut.
Spiral	(1) The result of twill weaving (under two, over two) continuously over an odd number of spokes. (2) A gradually widening curve winding away from a base to create a design.
Splice	The place where two pieces of wood, having been scarfed, overlap.
Spline	A wedge-shaped reed made primarily for use with pressed cane; also used to make loops and handles in baskets.
Splint	Strips of any wood thinned enough to use as stakes or weavers. Also called splits.
Split	See splint.
Spoke	The elements, usually round reed, which form the rigid framework of a basket.
Staining	A term that has come to mean coloring reed to give it an aged look.
Stake	Pieces of the woven mat (base) which are upsett and become the upright elements.
Stepping up	A term used in twill weaving meaning to start the next row one stake to the right (or left, as the case may be) of the starting point on the previous row.
Stroke	A movement of the weaver within the context of a weaving pattern; i.e., in the pattern over 4, under 3, over 4 is a stroke and under 3 is a stroke.
Swing handle	A handle attached to a basket by means of a loop or protruding ear that allows it to swing freely from side to side.
Three-point lashing	The wrapping used to cover the intersecting point of any three elements.
Three-rod wale	Inserting three weavers, each behind three consecutive stakes, with all three weaving, one at a time, over two and under one.
True	To measure the woven base, making sure all sides are the correct length, adjusting if necessary and marking corners.
Tucking in	When the basket is woven, the outside stakes are pointed, bent over and tucked into the weaving on the inside of the basket; also called down staking.
Twill	A method of weaving in which the weaver passes over and under the stakes two or three at a time.
Twining	A method of weaving (usually with round reed) using two or more elements that twist around each other as they weave around the spokes or stakes; also called pairing.
Two-point lashing	A wrapping used at the intersecting point of any two pieces.

Upsett or Upstake	To bend the stakes up and over upon themselves (toward the base), creating a crease at the base of the stake.
Wale	A method of weaving in which the left weaver is always moved over the weavers and spokes to the right, behind one and out to the front.
Warp	The stationary, usually more rigid, element in weaving.
Weaver	The fiber, often reed, used as the "weft" that moves over and under the stakes, spokes or ribs (warp).
Weft	The more flexible weaving element that is interlaced around the warp.
Wheat stitch	A two part V stitch used in coiling.
Wicker	From the Swedish vikker, meaning "willow" or "osier." Generally refers to any round, shoot-like material used for basketmaking.
Wicker work	A basketry technique that employs round, vertical stakes or spokes, and round weavers which are woven perpendicular to the spokes.
Willow	An osier which yields its long, slender branches for use in basket weaving and for making basket handles.
Wisteria	Climbing vine that is particularly flexible and is used alternately in a twisting pattern; in front of one spoke and behind one spoke.

Lyn Syler - Did you know Lyn taught high school English before she became a basketmaker?

Bibliography

Dyer, Wayne. *The Power of Intention, Learning to Co-create Your World Your Way,* 2004. Hay House Inc., PO Box 5100, Carlsbad, CA

Hoppe, Flo. *Contemporary Wicker Basketry,* 2005. 221 Dave Road, Rome, New York, 13440 - 1901

Izar, Suzanne S. and Jorgensen, Susan S. *Knitting into the Mystery: A Guide to the Shawl-Knitting Ministry,* 2003. Morehouse Publishing, PO Box 1321, Harrisburg, PA 17105

LaPlantz, Shereen. *Twill Basketry,* 1993. Lark Books, 64 Broadway, Asheville, NC 28801

Siler, Lyn. *The Basket Book,* 1988. Sterling Publishing Co., Inc. 387 Park Avenue South, New York, NY 10016

Siler, Lyn. *Handmade Baskets,* 1991. Sterling Publishing Co., Inc. 387 Park Avenue South, New York, NY 10016

Walker, Barbara G. *A Treasury of Knitting Patterns,* 1968. Charles Scribner's Sons, New York

Noted "Bibliobarkrapher", Geoffrey, Lyn's Weimaraner; seen here Hard at Work!